Contents

Acknowledgements   iv

Advisory Group   v

Preface   vi

1   **Introduction**   1
   Background   1
   Aims and scope of the research   3
   Research design and methods   3
   A period of transition   4
   Coverage of the report   5

2   **Issues of concern**   6
   Young people's concerns   6

3   **Interest in politics**   11
   Political interest across the sample   11
   What turns young people off politics   15
   Latchpoints that activate political interest   16
   Fostering and nurturing an interest in politics   17

4   **Images of politics, Parliament and politicians**   23
   Conceptions of politics   23
   Conceptions of Parliament   25
   Image of politicians   26
   Images of the politically interested   31
   Views about the Scottish Parliament   32

5   **Political engagement**   34
   What constitutes a political activity?   34
   Barriers to participating in politics   34
   How are young people engaging with the political process?   36
   Responses to the first voting opportunity   36
   Voting behaviour at the 1997 General Election   37

6   **Encouraging political interest**   40
   Making politics more interesting and accessible   40
   Changing politicians   42
   New opportunities for young people to participate in the political process   43
   Concluding remarks   43

References   47

Appendix 1: Technical appendix   49

Appendix 2: Topic guide   54

Acknowledgements

This study was made possible by a grant awarded by the Joseph Rowntree Foundation to whom we are very grateful. We are particularly indebted to our project managers, Charlie Lloyd and Pat Kneen, for their support and guidance throughout the project.

Special thanks are due also to the members of our Advisory Group, who kindly gave up considerable amounts of their time and, in many cases, travelled long distances to attend each meeting. They wisely informed our research strategy and played a key role in guiding and shaping the development of the project.

At the National Centre for Social Research we are very grateful to a number of people who were involved in the study. In the Qualitative Research Unit we would particularly like to thank Rachel Turner for her involvement in all aspects of the early stages of the research. We would also like to thank Kay Parkinson and Kit Ward, who carried out a number of the in-depth interviews and focus groups. Their skills in interviewing, and thoughtful and creative approach to the subject matter, have contributed greatly to the understanding gained from the study.

Finally, and most especially, we would like to thank all the people who took part in the research. We are grateful to them for giving their time and sharing their views about a subject that was not always high on their agenda in terms of interest.

Young people's politics
Political interest and engagement amongst 14–24 year olds

Clarissa White, Sara Bruce and Jane Ritchie

The **Joseph Rowntree Foundation** has supported this project as part of its programme of research and innovative development projects, which it hopes will be of value to policy makers and practitioners. The facts presented and views expressed in this report are, however, those of the authors and not necessarily those of the Foundation.

The **National Centre for Social Research** is Britain's largest independent non-profit institute for social research. Started in 1969 (as SCPR), its research work is funded by government departments, research councils, charitable foundations and other public bodies.

National Centre for Social Research, 35 Northampton Square, London EC1V OAX. Tel. 020 7250 1866

National Centre *for* Social Research

Formerly SCPR

© Joseph Rowntree Foundation 2000

Published for the Joseph Rowntree Foundation by YPS

ISBN 1 899987 64 4 ✔

Cover design by Adkins Design

Prepared and printed by:
York Publishing Services Ltd
64 Hallfield Road
Layerthorpe
York YO31 7ZQ
Tel: 01904 430033; Fax: 01904 430868; E-mail: orders@yps,ymn.co.uk

Advisory Group

Virginia Burton	Home Office
Caroline Clipson	British Youth Council
Professor John Curtice	University of Strathclyde
Dr Ian Davies	University of York
George Johnston	YouthLink Scotland
Richard Kimberlee	University of the West of England
Sally Loader	National Federation of Youth Action Agencies
Jan Newton	The Citizenship Foundation
Alison Park	National Centre for Social Research
Dr Alan Prout	University of Hull
Dr Debi Roker	Trust for the Study of Adolescence
Phil Treseder	Save the Children

Preface

It is known that young people have depressingly low levels of political interest and knowledge. They also have very poor opinions of politicians and parliamentary behaviour. This study set out to investigate the reasons why this is so, and to further explore young people's political views and behaviour.

A cross-section of young people, aged between 14 and 24, purposively selected from a diverse range of backgrounds and circumstances in England, Wales and Scotland, were consulted. They were invited to consider politics in their terms, employing their reference points as well as conventional political benchmarks. A research team from the Qualitative Research Unit at the National Centre for Social Research carried out the study. It was funded by a grant from the Joseph Rowntree Foundation.

The research demonstrates that young people cannot be treated as a uniform group where politics is concerned. Not surprisingly, they vary in their levels of interest in politics and display their interest in a variety of ways. But the evidence provides further understanding of how young people assess their interest in politics. It also shows how the interaction between the personal and financial circumstances of an individual, their beliefs and values, and a range of external factors, will determine how a young person conceptualises politics, which in turn influences the level of connection they make with it.

The findings both confirm and contribute to existing evidence about the factors that disengage political interest. First, because young people conceptualise politics in a limited and narrow way they perceive the subject as boring and irrelevant to their lives at present. Second,

their lack of knowledge and understanding about politics, and the difficulties they perceive in trying to grasp such a 'complex' and 'dull' subject, leave them with insufficient access to political matters. Third, their lack of trust in politicians to tell the truth, keep promises and be accountable has turned young people away from politics. Finally, the lack of opportunities for young people to engage in the political process until the age of 18, and the perceived failure of politicians to be responsive to the needs of young people, had also contributed to low levels of political interest.

In spite of apparently low levels of interest in politics, the issues that concern young people cover the broad political agenda, even if they are framed and spoken about in different terms. Furthermore, young people in the sample had engaged in a range of activities that were concerned with politics. Even people with little or no interest in politics had sometimes voted, or taken part in some other activity. Young people, however, consistently referred to the ways in which they are excluded from politics.

This report describes the key findings of the study. The first two chapters provide a context for the research, outlining the background to the study, its design and coverage, and a map of the issues that were of concern to young people. The following three chapters report on the participants' images and conceptions of Parliament and politicians, and their levels of political interest and engagement. The final chapter considers strategies for trying to kindle and nurture young people's involvement in the political and democratic process.

The study was qualitative in design in order to allow an exploratory and in-depth investigation of the political views and behaviours of young people. The small sample size and, more particularly, the way in which the sample was selected, mean that the study cannot provide any statistical data relating to the prevalence of views, experiences or behaviours. Where any such conclusions are suggested by the data, they are presented only as hypotheses to be tested.

1 Introduction

Background

During the 1990s media speculation and academic debate have been increasingly exercised over the alienation of young people from British political life. The notion that young people have low levels of political interest, knowledge and behaviour has been well documented (e.g. Furnham and Gunter, 1987; Mardle and Taylor, 1987; Park, 1995; Stradling, 1977). Recent concern, however, has focused on whether today's young are more disenchanted with politics than their predecessor generations. Research evidence suggests a decline in interest and engagement among young people (Park, 1999), but without reliable longitudinal data, it is not yet clear whether this has worrying implications for the future health of British democracy.

Several writers have claimed that a new kind of political generation is emerging, with young people rejecting conventional politics in favour of channelling their attention and energy to single issues, such as the environment, human and animal rights (e.g. Dubois, 1980; Mort, 1990; Wilkinson and Mulgan, 1995). Commentators have suggested that they have a distinct political agenda because of wider societal changes as opposed to political alienation or apathy (Inglehart, 1990; Wilkinson and Mulgan, 1995).

In contrast, 'life-cycle' explanations, as originally conceived by Butler and Stokes (1969), argue that political interest will increase with age and responsibility. Today's young, it is argued, like the generations before them, will acquire interest in politics as they grow older and as politics starts to have more relevance in their lives. The suggested decline in political interest and behaviour of young people, therefore, should be attributed to the changing social and economic environment in which young people now live. As entry into the workplace is increasingly deferred, there has been a prolonged dependence on parental support. It is suggested that this has delayed the onset of financial and familial responsibilities and, hence, the age at which people begin to become interested in politics (Kimberlee, 1998).

Research assessing young people's political interest and engagement has principally employed quantitative, rather than qualitative methods. In addition, researchers have tended to use rather narrow and conventional indicators of political interest, for example, by examining voting behaviour, party identification and knowledge of parliamentary politics. Such measures depend on the context in which questions are asked and the reference points used by young people to make their judgements. Without a clear understanding of how young people conceptualise political interest and engagement, it is difficult to know how they interpret such questions or the reasons for their responses.

Furthermore, much of the research on political attitudes and behaviour has tended to confine its focus to the disenfranchisement of particular sub-groups, such as unemployed young people (e.g. Banks and Ullah, 1987); or has restricted investigation to fairly narrow age bands, such as 15–16 year olds (Mardle and Taylor, 1987). Rather than addressing broader issues of interest or involvement, studies have tended to concentrate on particular issues, such as the political ignorance (Furnham and Gunter, 1987), or the political socialisation, of young people (e.g. Banks and Roker, 1994; Dawson *et al.*, 1977; Himmelweit *et al.*, 1981).

Other research in this field has consulted young people under broader banners, tapping both young people's social attitudes and values, as well as their political attitudes and beliefs (e.g. Park, 1999; Wilkinson and Mulgan, 1995). These studies have a wider focus but have predominantly attempted quantitative measurement of the political attitudes and behaviour of the young. The political interest and activity of the young has also been explored more tangentially, in studies about citizenship (Richardson, 1990) and social exclusion (Bentley and Oakley, 1999).

Typical explanations for the lack of interest in politics include young people's belief that politics lacks relevance for them or their preoccupation with other interests and concerns. Other studies point to the complexity of politics and the difficulties young people have in understanding political life and processes. With the exception of work carried out by Park[1] (1999), young people have also been found to hold politicians in low esteem, lacking trust in them (Bentley and Oakley, 1999), or respect for them (Pririe and Worcester, 1998). This too is identified as a disincentive to become interested in politics.

Research which challenges the image of young people as alienated and disaffected has uncovered a high level of voluntary and campaigning activity amongst 14 and 16 year olds (Roker *et al.* 1997). Bhavnani's (1991) ethnographic study raised the possibility that young people could be involved in activities that they themselves would not define as politics, but which could be placed within a broad domain of political interest. Similarly, some of the participants in a study by Richardson (1990) had been involved in activities or committees at school, but rarely saw this as political activity.

The reasons why young people do, or do not, participate in political activities is not well understood. Richardson (1990), for example, argues that politicians are not interested in the views of young people. Jowell and Park (1998) suggest that their lack of participation results from other preoccupations and interests, such as finding partners, homes and jobs. Marsh (1989) argues that broader social changes are undermining the extent to which existing institutions inform young people's political beliefs and actions. He claims that de-industrialisation, the demise of trade unions, and social and geographical mobility have all had an effect on the traditional political socialisation of young people.

There has been increasing concern that schools are not doing enough to educate children about political institutions and processes. Since the introduction of the National Curriculum, politics has only been covered in an *ad hoc* manner, as the 1998 Education Reform Act did not require schools to have any central responsibility for civic and political education. Following the Crick Report in 1998, which provided guidelines for effective education for citizenship, it was announced in 1999 that citizenship will become a compulsory subject for 11–16 year olds after September 2002. It is planned that this will include learning about proportional representation, the operation of Parliament, resolving moral dilemmas and ways to participate in community service. At primary school, citizenship lessons will be part of existing courses in personal, social and health education (PSHE). But in the absence of a better understanding of young people's interests and requirements, such proposals may be difficult to implement.

A review of the existing literature reveals that there is still a lack of understanding about how the young view the political world, both the political institutions and the people who operate them. It is also not clear what aspects of politics – either in a conventional or broader sense – interest young people. Furthermore, there is insufficient knowledge about the ways in which the young do, or do not, engage in the civic process. Given there is such concern about the disconnection of the young from politics, and the implications this will have on future democratic practice, there is a need to understand these issues in much greater depth.

This qualitative study provides further understanding of young people's political interests and behaviours. It portrays their perspectives, using their terminology and language, thereby helping to frame the debate about the nature of young people's political interest and engagement in ways that are meaningful to them.

Aims and scope of the research

The research explored in detail how young people view the world of politics. No attempt was made to impose a definition of politics during the study. Instead, the young people were invited to consider politics in the broadest sense, in their own terms, so as to avoid orientating them to more conventional notions of politics.

The study included two groups of young people: first-time voters at the 1997 general election and those who will be the next generation of first-time voters. It involved young people living in the UK, aged between 14 and 24 years, covering those who were in education, training, employment or unemployment.

The key objectives of the research were to:

- generate a map of the issues and concerns that young people have, and to compare these with the issues with which they believe politicians are concerned

- explore the way in which young people conceptualise politics, considering the images they have of Parliament, politicians and the areas which politics covers

- investigate the nature of young people's political interest and engagement, and the factors which have influenced or motivated their engagement or disengagement with politics

- pinpoint ways in which young people could be encouraged to take more interest in, or be more engaged with, politics.

Research design and methods

The research was qualitative in design and employed a combination of 24 focus groups, 16 paired and 20 individual interviews. These were structured across four different age groups, covering those aged 14–15, 16–17, 18–20 and 21–24 years. A total of 193 young people took part.

As this was a qualitative study, the rationale for sample selection was not to select a statistically representative sample of all young people, but to ensure diversity of coverage across certain key variables. Eligibility for the study was determined using a household screen and quotas were set in order to prescribe the distribution of the sample selected. These ensured diverse coverage within the following variables:

- age

- gender

- ethnic origin

- social class, as determined by the parent's occupation for participants up to the age of 18 years

- current educational or employment activity

- highest educational attainment

- interest in politics

- voting behaviour of those over the age of 18 years.

The sample was selected across ten locations in Scotland, England and Wales.

A set of verbatim transcripts was produced from the tape recordings of the interviews and the focus groups. Analysis was undertaken using 'Framework', a qualitative analytic method developed at the National Centre for Social Research (Ritchie and Spencer, 1994). Further details of the design and conduct of the study are given in Appendix 1. A copy of the topic guide can be seen in Appendix 2.

Profile of the sample

The purposive nature of the sample selection ensured the sampling criteria were met across all variables and that young people from a wide range of different circumstances and backgrounds were included in the study. As a consequence, the sample was composed of virtually equal numbers of males and females across the four age groups. Just over half the study participants were in full-time education – studying either GCSEs or Scottish Standard grades, further or higher education qualifications. About a quarter of the sample were in paid employment, either full-time or part-time or self-employed. The remainder were unemployed or on a government programme.

In terms of educational attainment, just under one-third of the sample had no qualifications, or fewer than five GCSEs grades A–C, or five Scottish Standard grades A–C, or vocational equivalents. A further third had five or more GCSEs grades A–C, or five Scottish Standard grades A–C, or vocational equivalents. About a quarter had A Levels/Advanced GNVQs, or Scottish Highers and the remainder had higher education qualifications, including first degrees, HND and BTEC Diplomas.

Approximately four-fifths of the sample were white, while the remaining fifth were distributed across a range of minority ethnic groups. Just under two-thirds of the sample lived in locations in England or Wales, with just over one-third living in Scotland[2]. The profile of the sample is shown in Appendix 1.

A period of transition

The 11 year span between 14 and 24 years, covered in this study, represents a time of considerable change for young people, as they progress from childhood to early adulthood. Across the different age groups, developments were occurring in all domains of the young people's lives – occupational, social, familial and financial. The effects that such changing personal circumstances had on views about politics were explored in the research.

As young people progressed along their educational paths, some changed institutions, moving from school to college, or to university. Along other routes, people moved between education, employment and unemployment. Sometimes these transitions coincided with young people acquiring new roles and responsibilities, such as leaving the parental home and assuming greater personal and financial independence. In some cases young people had started a family, and this had brought with it new responsibilities and influences. Others were acquiring new friendships and partnerships that resulted in different influences on their values, behaviours and attitudes, including those related to politics.

As will be seen throughout the report these changing personal circumstances influenced the way in which young people connected and engaged with politics. They have a bearing on the types of issues that were of interest and concern to them, the way in which they conceptualised politics, the nature and level of their interest in politics, and the degree to which they participated in political processes.

Coverage of the report

The remainder of the report documents the research findings. Chapter 2 considers some of the issues that were of concern to young people.

Chapter 3 reports levels of political interest held across the sample and the important 'latchpoints' for, or deterrents to, fostering political interest. Chapter 4 covers young people's images and conceptions of Parliament and politicians, and Chapter 5 looks at levels of political engagement. The final chapter considers strategies for trying to kindle and nurture young people's involvement in the political and democratic process.

The report uses verbatim quotations and case illustrations throughout. Where necessary, details of the contributors, or their subjects, have been moderately changed to protect anonymity. Pseudonyms have also been used.

The small sample size and, most particularly, the purposive nature of the sample selection, means that the study cannot provide any statistical data relating to the prevalence of views, experiences, or behaviours. Where any such conclusions are suggested by the data, they are presented only as hypotheses to be tested.

Notes

1   Park (1999) reported that 12–19 year olds have a higher level of trust in politicians than their adult counterparts.

2   In order to ensure that separate analysis could be carried out in Scotland, the sample was designed to include coverage of all four age groups across the key variables.

2 Issues of concern

This chapter reports on the issues that were of concern to young people. These covered a wide range of issues. Although interest in 'single issues', such as the environment or animal protection, was raised these were by no means the dominant concerns voiced. Moreover, while the young people seldom mentioned politics explicitly, a number of issues raised are clearly matters of concern to politicians and can be labelled political issues. Indeed, young people were sometimes surprised to discover common themes between their interests and those of politicians. They did, however, distinguish between the differing terms of reference employed by politicians and by young people, even if the broad subject areas overlapped.

Young people's concerns

There were four different levels – personal, local, national, and global – within the map of concerns generated by young people (Figure 1). These reflect the ways in which an issue was expressed – ranging from a concern with an individual's personal circumstances, their local community, or with those of national or global significance.

In general, there was considerable overlap between the range of issues identified across the sample. However, the ways in which these issues were expressed evolved in response to the life-stage they had reached. This was evident both in terms of the nature of the concern and the breadth of focus with which it was described. For example, an issue like education was important to young people of all ages, but the nature of their concern reflected changing experiences in relation to their own education. Similarly, issues that were solely

rooted in personal or local worlds for the youngest sample members, started to assume national, and sometimes global, perspectives amongst older age groups.

Individuals from all age groups cited the following concerns.

Education

Education was an important issue for all young people. For young people under 16 years, concerns revolved around bullying, being overloaded with homework, the pressure to pass exams and treatment by teachers. The focus for young people aged between 17 and 18 years was on the pressures of taking exams and successfully achieving qualifications. Young people over the age of 18 seemed to have three main concerns, the variable standards of education, the cost of education and pressures involved in acquiring qualifications to pursue a particular career path or enter higher education.

These concerns operated at both the personal and national level. At the personal level, for example, they related to financial difficulties resulting from paying for higher education since grants had been cut. Lack of funding was also raised at the national level, in relation to the range of facilities and courses open to young people.

Employment

The issue of employment was raised at local, personal and national levels. Not surprisingly, it was a more important issue for young people over the age of 16. There were three main areas of concern, all of which revolved around the insecure nature of the labour market and high levels of unemployment. There were felt to be few opportunities and limited choices for young people who left full-time compulsory education

Figure 1 Map of young people's concerns

Local

Labour market
Lack of social facilities
Drug use and pushers
Crime and violence
Policing strategies
Family planning advice
Unreliable transport provision

Personal

School/college experience
Acquiring qualifications
Job availability and security
Lack of money
Social life
Discrimination
Drug and alcohol use
Personal safety
Relationships
Treatment of young people
Keeping fit and healthy
Self image/identity
Under-age sex
Invasion of privacy

Global

Relations with other countries
Wars
Conditions in other countries
Nationalism and devolution
Protection of the environment
Preservation of wildlife

National

Education
Employment
Economy
Discrimination
Drug laws and education
Crime and justice
Age limits
Housing
Environment
Animal cruelty
Transport policy
Government and politics
Media

at 16; limited opportunities for training and apprenticeships, which also restricted further job opportunities and prospects; and concerns about the way in which employers treat young people, in particular, poor working conditions and low pay.

Finance

Lack of money was another issue raised by all age groups. However, the frame of reference differed depending on the life-stage reached by a young person. For example, young people under 18 were concerned with their lack of money to fund leisure and social activities, and other material acquisitions. Those over 18 shared such concerns, but also worried about being able to support themselves independently after leaving the parental home. In addition, young people who had become parents were concerned with being able to financially support their families.

At the national level, the economy was discussed and concerns typically revolved around the amount of tax the government levies, and the nature of items on which it is raised. This was noted particularly by those who were paying income tax, tax on cigarettes and alcohol, or petrol and road tax. Other concerns related to the way government allocates its resources and, in particular, the allocation for public sector spending.

Social and leisure facilities

The lack of social and leisure facilities was a recurrent issue for young people under the age of 20, but particularly for those under 18 years. Facilities such as youth clubs, which do exist for young people of this age group, were either perceived as being in short supply, or too boring to visit. The choice available was further restricted by age restrictions for alcohol consumption. As a result, it was claimed that young people were inclined to collect on the streets, with the resulting possibility of getting involved in crime. A few people over 20 years raised lack of facilities and their concerns were usually in relation to their children.

Discrimination

All age groups raised discrimination against particular groups in society. Both white people and those from minority ethnic communities discussed this issue at all levels. Concerns about racism focused on the personal safety of members of minority ethnic groups; the need for protection from violence and abuse were both raised. This had both personal relevance, as well as being of significance nationally, in relation to incidents like the murder of Stephen Lawrence. At the national level, it was felt that there should be equality of opportunity and treatment for all members of society. While racial discrimination was the central concern, there were also references to discrimination on grounds of sex and disability.

Substance use and abuse

The use of substances was recurrently raised by all age groups. It was primarily discussed in relation to drugs, but alcohol use and smoking were also mentioned by the youngest members of the sample. There was some concern about the negative side effects of drugs, such as crime and HIV, the ease with which young people can get access to drugs and the need for more information about drug use. A distinction, however, was sometimes drawn between the sorts of drugs which are harmful and addictive, and those which it is implied are less harmful and are more recreationally used. Some discussed their enjoyment of using drugs and their positive benefits in relieving stress. The legalisation of cannabis was also noted.

Concerns about alcohol and smoking were raised in relation to age limits and not being able to obtain these items, as well as the harm caused by drinking or smoking in excess.

Crime

The issue of crime was raised in a similar way by all age groups. Personal safety and the ability to go out alone or at night seemed to be the key concern for young people. General wariness about personal safety seemed to have been driven primarily by a perception that there was a lot of crime, combined with a lack of policing in the local area. Other more specific concerns, raised by young people over 18 years, related to the criminal justice system and perceptions that sentencing policy was applied inconsistently.

Relationships

A common concern across the sample was the ability to form and maintain relationships with friends and partners. Mostly, concerns related to the way in which relationships were changing as young people entered different life stages, and encountered new situations and environments. Worries about loneliness was a key issue, particularly how they would cope with moving out of the parental home and forming new friendships and relationships, but also settling down, having a family and forming stable partnerships. The youngest participants were also concerned about the pressure exercised by parents on young people to behave in a particular way, or to work hard at school.

Treatment of young people

The judgmental and negative way in which young people were felt to be regarded and treated was an issue that exercised young people across the sample. Young people under 16 years referred to the way in which they are sometimes treated with suspicion by teachers at school, or with a parental lack of trust at home. The number and range of ways in which their freedoms are curbed by various age limits imposed upon them further compounded feelings of marginalisation. Young people over 16 talked about the way in which older people seem reluctant to invest trust or responsibility in young people.

Health

While health was an issue raised by members of all age groups, concern seemed to increase with age. It was also a matter that had personal and national relevance. Concerns about health primarily related to the need for personal health and fitness when young, but there was also some reference to their health in old age. Health was discussed at the national level in terms of the shortage of funding for the NHS, which had implications for the number of doctors, nurses and beds available, the quality of service received and the cost of prescriptions.

The environment

The environment was primarily a concern at the national and global level. While it was raised by individuals in all age groups, it seemed to be of less concern than some of the above issues. Tackling pollution, preventing global warming, stemming urban development and encouraging people to recycle were among the issues noted.

International relations

At the global level, young people cited concerns to do with relations with other countries; poverty, Third World debt and wars in different parts of the globe (e.g. Bosnia, Iraq and Africa). At the national level, the need for devolution in Scotland, but also in Wales, was identified by young people living in these countries. A wish for an end to the troubles in Northern Ireland was also expressed.

Further issues

In addition to the above subjects, a number of other less commonly cited concerns were raised. Housing issues were raised, in connection with finding affordable accommodation and the provision of housing for the homeless. Animal protection was raised, in relation to the cruel way in which animals are treated and used in experiments. At the global level concerns related to preservation of wildlife in other countries. Concerns about the difficulties young people face growing up, included coming to terms with an individual's sexuality, trying to conform to the perfect body image and the pressure to have under-age sex. In addition, there were worries about the number of teenage pregnancies and the lack of family planning services. Other more exceptional concerns raised included government performance, the actions of politicians, the high cost and unreliability of public transport, media intrusion of public privacy, the role of media in encouraging violence among children, euthanasia and the influence of religion on young people.

3 Interest in politics

This chapter explores levels of political interest across the sample. It provides further understanding of the different ways in which young people connect with politics, identifying the factors which shape and inform their levels of interest. It also traces the process through which interest in politics develops and the catalysts that activate such developments.

Political interest across the sample

As noted in Chapter 1, the rationale for sample selection was not to select a statistically representative sample of all young people, but to ensure diversity of coverage across levels of political interest. At the recruitment stage, just over two-fifths of the sample reported having 'no interest' in politics, another two-fifths had 'some interest' in politics and just over one-tenth had 'quite a lot of interest' in politics. Not surprisingly, once young people were invited to explore their interest in politics in a more expansive way, during the interviews and groups discussions, they sometimes assessed their levels of interest differently. As a consequence, there was some variation between reported levels of political interest at the recruitment stage and that described by young people during the groups and interviews. For example, according to the latter assessment just under two-thirds reported having no interest in politics.

Based on the group and interview data, young people have been classified into five broad groups, according to their declared level of interest in politics and how they amplified and explained their level of connection with politics:

- Group 1 – Indifferent
- Group 2 – Cynically uninterested
- Group 3 – Selectively interested
- Group 4 – Generically interested
- Group 5 – Highly interested and connected

The groups characterise a spectrum of political interest within which movement can occur. Because of the small sample base and the purposive design of the sample, the internal distribution of the groups has no statistical significance. That said, young people under 18 were more common in the uninterested, rather than the interested groups. Apart from age, there were only slight differences in the way the groups were composed, although interest in politics did seem to increase with educational attainment.

Unconnected and uninterested – Groups 1 and 2

Two of the Groups, 1 and 2, lack any interest in, or connection with, politics. They are united in their dislike of politics and share a general perception that politics is boring. However, they display their lack of connection in different ways.

Group 1 – Indifferent

Group 1, or the indifferent group, appear to take no notice of politics and seem almost oblivious to it as a subject. They attribute their lack of interest in, and boredom with, politics to its lack of relevance within their lives. In general, they conceive of politics in fairly limited terms, usually focusing on negative stereotypes of

Case 1: Indifferent

Tracy, 20 years old, is working as an administrator for a large organisation in a small town. She lives in a housing association property, with her boyfriend who is working as a labourer. In her spare time she goes to a gym and swims. Politics for Tracy is 'everything' the 'Government, Tony Blair, things that are going on'. Her image of Parliament is of old men in suits, smoking cigars, sitting in big padded chairs with big desks. Tracy is 'not really fussed one way or the other' when it comes to politics. She lacks any knowledge about the subject, indicating that politics was not discussed at school, at home with her parents or with her boyfriend.

Tracy maintains that politics appeals to intelligent people because it is 'very complicated'. They are 'more likely to want to find out … what's going on in the world' rather than other people like herself who are more complacent about their lives.

Despite saying it is something she would like to know about when she decides to vote, she also confesses that 'it's not something that I'd … really want to find out about'.

Tracy said she could not 'be bothered' to vote in the 1997 election, in part also because she did not know who to vote for.

Case 2: Cynically uninterested

Michael is about to leave school to join the RAF. He is 16 years old and lives at home with his parents in Scotland. In addition to working part-time in a hotel, he cycles and plays snooker and hockey in his spare time. He is also a member of the Air Cadets.

As soon as Michael hears the word 'politics' his mind 'shuts down' because it's so 'boring' and has so little relevance for him. He argues, at 'our age we want to go out and have fun, [we] don't want to watch people sitting in a green and brown room having a debate about something that we can't argue with or agree with'. He does not talk about politics at home and decided against doing Modern Studies. Politicians, for Michael, are old, male and wealthy. They are also likely to have been high achievers at school. He is cynical about politicians because they take no interest in the views of young people. He also attributes his lack of faith to their failure to keep their promises or to 'change anything'.

He finds it difficult to see why he should take an interest in politics 'Because right now, it doesn't matter what we say, nothing will happen because we're too young to vote … so why should we be interested in it if it doesn't concern us, and we can't do anything about it.'

Michael imagined that he might become more interested once politics started to affect him and once he could actually vote, but even then he presumed he would find it dull.

Case 3: Selectively interested

Anna, 17 years, lives with her mother in a flat in London. Currently she volunteers at a youth centre, although she is about to study English at university. She also sits on a youth council, in order to ensure young people's voices are heard.

Even though Anna believes that politics is important, because it affects every aspect of people's lives, she equates the term with corruption and the way in which politicians 'want to rule our lives'. She is cynical about whether politicians are interested in 'what we want', because they are too preoccupied with 'money', 'power' and in serving themselves.

With the exception of issues which are of concern to Anna, she is bored by politics, 'because they're just talking about the same things, they're not doing nothing, they're not acting on it'. She also hates being 'under someone's thumb'. 'You've got them in their 60 grand a year job telling us, who ain't earning much, what our lives are going to be about.' She does, however, like to keep abreast of current affairs.

Because of her uncertainty about who to vote for Anna thinks she is unlikely to vote. But she also believes in taking a principled stance against British involvement in various wars, most recently in Bosnia.

politicians and their behaviour. They tend to find politics difficult to understand and show no willingness to engage with it as a subject because they are preoccupied with various leisure and social pursuits, which take precedence in their lives.

Group 2 – Cynically uninterested
Group 2 holds a more cynical view. While they display similarly negative conceptions of politics, they tend to actively avoid engaging with politics at home, school or through the media. They express their cynicism through their mistrust of, and lack of respect for, politicians. They justify their lack of interest in politics in terms of the way young people are excluded from the political process. This is experienced in two main ways: first, their perception that politicians lack interest in the

views of young people; and second, the limited opportunities that exist for young people to engage in politics until the age of 18.

Group 3 – Selectively interested
Group 3 are selectively interested in politics and only take an interest in politics when it relates to an issue of concern. Otherwise, they share similar views about politics as the previous two groups. A wide range of issues aroused their interest in politics: some had direct personal relevance, such as funding for Higher Education; others were driven by a 'social conscience', rather than self interest, although some may also have had some level of personal relevance. Examples included various national policy areas, such as funding for the NHS, homelessness, employment opportunities; issues connected with wider crusades, such as

human or animal rights, Third World poverty and protection of the environment; and some nationalist issues, which were concerned with Scottish and Welsh devolution.

This group expressed their interest in a variety of ways, either through a stated commitment and active pursuit of a particular concern; or more passively through, for example, following media and other coverage about developments within the field of interest.

Group 4 – Generically interested

Group 4 has a more generic interest in politics and range from those who have a slight or passing interest in politics, to those whose interest is more substantial. They tend to be at an early stage in the development of their views and opinions about politics. The focus of their interest tends to be general current affairs, rather than parliamentary politics, although the latter may interest them, for example, at election time, or when an issue which affects them is being debated and considered. This group tends to be more passively interested in politics than the previous group. As with the previous group,

they may take an interest in a range of issues, but these generally have direct personal relevance for the individual concerned. Among those mentioned were: an interest in tax levels for those in work, or an interest in issues connected with childcare and education for parents.

Group 5 – Highly interested and connected

The final group is the most interested in politics and have been classified as 'very interested'. They range from those who take quite a lot of interest, to those who report being 'fascinated' or 'passionate' about politics. They display a much higher level of commitment and interest in politics than all the other groups. The focus of their interest is varied and ranges from following parliamentary politics in some detail, to reading about and sometimes actively pursuing a range of political, constitutional and international issues. They may also be concerned with the structure and organisation of central and local government, political history, political theory and processes.

Case 4: Generically interested

Angela, 19 years, is living on her own in council accommodation. She left school at 16 to work in a computer firm, but has recently had to stop work because of falling ill while pregnant. When she was younger she was preoccupied with going out and 'having a good time' thereby having little time for, or interest in, politics.

Angela's interest in politics was stimulated by discussions with her parents about voting once she reached the age of 18. Even though she finds politics hard to understand she has started to take more notice of the news and current affairs in order to keep in touch with developments in politics. Because of her own circumstances, being pregnant and unable to work due to ill health, she takes a particular interest in money and health issues. However, she lacks trust in politicians to keep their promises as they are, as she sees it, too busy point scoring.

Case 5: Highly interested

Peter, 21 years, is in the final year of his Politics degree. Having also taken Politics at GCSE and A-level, he will have studied the subject for eight years. He believes that it is imperative that people of his age get involved with politics, at a local and a national level, as he maintains that Britain suffers too much from apathy. He is interested in the subject because 'society, everyday life is dominated by politics'.

His wish to study politics arose because he made a connection with the subject at an early age and when 'you feel strongly about something, it can be interesting'. He gets his information about politics from his university course, newspapers, news and current affairs programmes. Having studied politics for some time, he indicates a theoretical understanding and has formed strong opinions about the nature of the political system.

What turns young people off politics

The young people had a lot to say about the various features and factors that turned them away from politics. Finding politics boring was a consistently cited reason for not taking notice of, or being interested in, politics. While, for some, the mere mention of the word 'politics' was a deterrent, others attributed their boredom to specific issues. The way in which politics was delivered had left some with the impression that politics is dull, serious and monotonous. This was observed from the level of argument and discussion in Parliament, the content of speeches and the length of time it takes to achieve anything in the political world.

Underpinning this boredom, however, was a perception that politics lacks relevance to their lives at present. Indeed, it was commonly said that young people are preoccupied with other interests and activities, which dominate their lives, thereby leaving little time to devote to politics. This view was driven by a conception that politics was for older, more responsible, people whose lives are affected by politics. The point at which this was perceived to start varied from the age of 18 to the late 20s.

> It just looks boring and it doesn't do anything for me. At my age I don't want to know about that sort of thing, I don't want to know about voting and politics … I just want to get on with my life. (Female, 14 years, Cynically uninterested)

> There's nothing appealing about politics to young folk. (Male, 17 years, Cynically uninterested)

A lack of knowledge and understanding about politics and the perceived difficulties in trying to grasp such a complex subject had also turned some young people away from politics. They frequently expressed difficulty in comprehending the language used in politics, both the jargon and long, complex words. To take an interest in politics was seen to require a technical knowledge about concepts and ideas, which they found difficult to grasp. Sometimes this was thought to be because young people were not exposed to information about politics, either in their homes or at school. Other times, however, it resulted from young people choosing to 'switch off' from information about politics, almost whenever they were exposed to it.

15

It's of absolutely no interest to us ... You can't understand half what they're saying ... when they're like doing their little debates, they're just shouting and you can't understand a word they're saying. (Female, 15 years, Cynically uninterested)

I just haven't got a clue about politics at all ... for starters the vocabulary they use ... they talk in a different language. (Male, 20 years, Indifferent)

A lack of trust in politicians to tell the truth, keep their promises and be accountable had also turned some young people off politics. References were made to the way in which politicians were felt instead to pursue their own self-interest and gain. Reports of the way in which politicians sometimes behaved in their personal lives was also acknowledged as being a factor. However, this was also said to have entertained some young people and been a reason why they took an, albeit negative, interest in politics.

Politicians' lack of interest in the views and concerns of young people was another recurrent factor. It was consistently said that politicians fail to respond to, or address young people's concerns, as they are too selfishly concerned with their own agenda. As will be seen in the penultimate chapter, the belief that there was nothing that young people could do to register a view was sometimes used as a justification for political apathy.

They don't listen. They don't listen at all. They don't see it. They know what [young people] want but they don't do nothing about it. (Male, 16 years, Cynically uninterested)

When it comes to politics you might well just forget it because ... they're never going to listen and even if they pretend to listen ... they'll [say]

... oh, thank you for that, we'll look into it, and that's it. (Female, 17 years, Selectively interested)

Even where young people do express their wishes, either through voting or involving themselves in other activities to register their views, it is perceived as being accorded with little status by politicians.

The image of politicians is discussed in the following chapter but the mystique and ceremony which surrounds their activities had further conveyed the impression that politicians were remote from young people.

Whilst politicians' apparent lack of interest was an issue for young people in general, it had particular relevance for Scottish young people. They felt that Westminster was dominated by English politicians, who unfairly advantaged English and Welsh interests over Scottish interests. In addition, the geographical distance of Westminster prevented them having access to politicians and to Parliament, and had therefore further contributed to feelings of exclusion.

The lack of opportunities for young people to engage in politics until the age of 18 was also identified as another disincentive for being interested in politics.

You often think you can't do much about it, so you just get on with it and leave it up to the adults and then maybe when we're 18 we can decide who we'd like to vote for. (Male, 15 years, Indifferent)

Latchpoints that activate political interest

Three key latchpoints were identified as having activated an interest in politics for young people.

First, the growing relevance of politics

within an individual's life. Commonly this occurred as a result of changing personal circumstances, which often coincided with young people taking on new roles and responsibilities, which had brought them in contact with some aspect of politics. A key time seemed to be the point when young people assumed financial responsibility, or became 'stakeholders' for their own affairs, for example, moving out of the parental home, starting a job, or a family.

> When you get your own house it's like you become an adult. Before you get a house I always used to think: 'Oh, it's an old person's thing to look at'. You wouldn't sit down and watch [politics] – you'd turn over and watch something else. (Male, 22 years, Generically interested)

Second, being exposed to information about politics. Some young people mentioned acquiring an interest in politics as a result of discussions at home with their parents, or through a course at school or college. Otherwise it was said to have occurred through television coverage of an issue or event that had 'struck a chord' or aroused an interest.

> I saw a video on Bosnia … it has probably been the most horrible thing I've ever seen in my life and it really … woke me up [to politics] … I just couldn't believe this was happening in the world. (Male, 24 years, Very interested)

Occasionally, a friend, colleague or 'role model' had been instrumental in informing a young person about the subject and stimulating their interest.

Third, the opportunity to engage in politics. Electoral eligibility and the desire to fulfil a civic responsibility or duty was the key trigger to arousing interest. Other types of activities, however, were also identified as, sometimes, having a similar effect. These included joining a society, joining a youth forum or schools council, or embarking on a campaign in support of a particular issue. Constitutional change, such as Scottish and Welsh devolution, was also identified as being a stimulant to an interest in politics.

> I'll be more interested when Scotland gets their own [Parliament] … we actually have some chance of doing something that'll actually affect us directly. … hopefully it'll become more relevant to me personally. (Male 18 years, Generically interested)

Fostering and nurturing an interest in politics

The process in which political interest is acquired and shaped will involve the interaction between the personal and financial circumstances of an individual, their beliefs and values, and a range of external factors that shape and influence interest in politics. The way in which these inter-connect will determine how a young person conceptualises politics, which in turn influences the level of connection they make with politics. The level of connection that is made with politics will then, in turn, determine the way in which they engage with information they receive about politics. The process is cyclical, as Figure 2 illustrates.

Depending on an individual's personal circumstances, they will be networked into a range of different, but related, lines of information about politics, each of which will have the potential to make an impact. As can be

Figure 2 Fostering and nurturing political interest

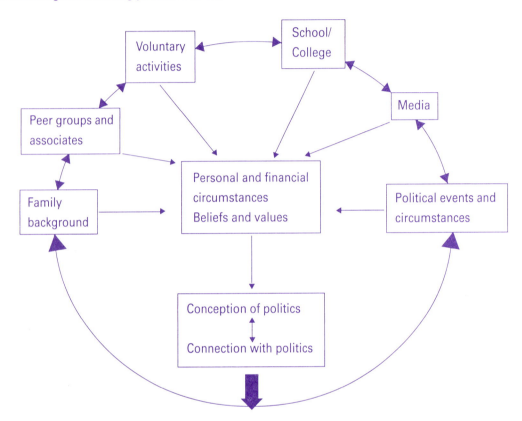

seen from Figure 2, young people identified five main sources of information about politics, although clearly there are others that may be influential.

Family background – the experience of being brought up in a family where there is some level of political discussion and interest at home does seem to have a bearing on young people's interest in politics (Himmelweit *et al.*, 1981). Political discussion had arisen in the context of general discussions with parents and other family members, when young people sought clarification about an issue to do with politics, or when young people were present whilst their parents were watching the news, or some other programme connected with politics.

Well I think [my interest in politics] *it's got a lot to do with the way you're brought up ... there seems to be a time in childhood when you start asking questions about everything, suddenly everything from God down to parental relationships ... and realising the truth behind* [them]. (Female, 19 years, Very interested)

In addition, parents had encouraged young people to engage politically either, for example, through signing petitions, or through taking part in demonstrations or, as will be seen in Chapter 5, through voting.

Peer groups and associates seemed to be a less commonly cited source of information about politics, although the extent to which young people engaged in discussions about politics varied. Young people in the interested groups did sometimes report discussing politics with friends, or colleagues on courses. The topic of their discussions varied from focusing on a particular political issue or topical news event to a subject which related to some aspect of a course they were undertaking. Sometimes young people talked about having heated political discussions with friends. However, if the conversation was likely to result in an argument then this was sometimes deemed to be a reason for avoiding discussing politics with friends.

Young people identified a range of different ways in which politics had been taught at school and college. These included formal classes about politics, which were incorporated into either PSHE or Modern Studies, as well as discussions about politics as part of another course, such as History, Law or Sociology. As part of these various courses, they sometimes had been encouraged to write to politicians, or to take part in a mock election. In addition, some young people had elected to pursue a course in politics. The content of these different courses and activities ranged from learning about the British political system, the organisation and structure of government, the role of MPs, the legislative process, party politics, various social and economic issues, electoral systems and international politics. Various extracurricular activities also involved young people in trips to Parliament, presentations from visiting speakers about political issues or parties, discussions during assembly and participation in schools councils or, in an exceptional case, a political debating club. Other activities, such as fundraising or campaigning projects in support of local issues

or charities, also brought young people in contact with politics.

Young people cited the media as one of the main sources of information about politics, although their willingness to engage with it varied. It seemed that some of the negative images that young people had about politics and politicians (see Chapter 4) had arisen from the media. Media coverage of politics was also sometimes perceived as being framed around party political squabbles in Parliament. This reinforced the view that politics is boring, but also appeared to have narrowed the way in which the subject was conceptualised.

Political events and circumstances sometimes seemed to have aroused an awareness of politics. Where discussed, examples included exposure to a topical issue or event, such as the war in Bosnia and Kosovo, or as a result of being brought up in a country where there was a heightened political awareness, such as Northern Ireland. It was also mentioned by some of the Scottish and Welsh sample, who were responding to ongoing political developments within their countries.

Finally, participation in various voluntary activities, such as a youth forum, and campaigning groups or organisations, such as animal welfare charities or organisations safeguarding human rights, had also raised awareness about politics and sometimes brought young people directly into contact with politicians.

As will be seen, the degree to which these influences will foster and nurture an interest in politics will depend upon the degree to which an individual is open to receiving information about politics. It will also depend upon whether young people believe that the information they receive is easy to understand and has some relevance within their lives. Not surprisingly, these factors operated differently across the sample, particularly across the politically interested groups.

The politically uninterested groups – Groups 1 and 2

Group 1 and, to a lesser extent, Group 2 tend to have a fairly limited understanding of politics. Their conception of politics appeared to revolve around fairly superficial hooks, such as the performance and visual image of various politicians. They seem to have had little or no exposure to politics at home or at school, or else claim to have actively avoided the exposure because they found politics too drab and boring, or too complex to understand. Where they have been involved in discussions at home, it seemed to have influenced and reinforced negative conceptions of politics.

On the whole neither group discusses politics with their friends, although conversations about the budget and voting decisions had exceptionally occurred. These young people are also unlikely to watch anything political on the television or read any political coverage in a newspaper.

At present neither group entertains an interest in politics, although there is some recognition that an interest may develop in the future. In order to stimulate the interest of the indifferent group it seems that something has to change in their personal circumstances which will encourage them to reappraise their negative conception of politics. This group lacks understanding about politics, they may therefore be open to information which is delivered in an accessible and interesting way.

But, unless they are convinced of the relevance and applicability of these messages within their lives, these cues and messages will continue to be blanked. They assumed this might occur when greater financial responsibility and independence came. They also suggested that reaching the age of electoral eligibility, for those under 18, might be a catalyst for their interest. In this way members of this group may be contenders for developing into people with a generic interest in politics.

The prognosis for Group 2, however, does not seem so promising and they are likely to be the hardest to engage in politics. They are more cynical about politics and also more mistrustful of politicians, therefore they may not change their conception of politics even when it starts to affect them. They are also likely to be more resistant than the indifferent group to receiving information about politics. Since they believe that young people are excluded from politics, politicians need to persuade them that they are addressing and responding to young people's issues and concerns. However, as they have effectively switched off to messages about politics it is difficult to see how politicians will be able to convince them of this. Nevertheless, it is clear that interest in politics may be stimulated for some of the younger members of this group when they reach electoral age.

The politically interested groups – Groups 3, 4 and 5

Among the interested groups, views were being shaped and informed by a range of different sources of information about politics, such as through discussions with family members or friends, at school or college, and voluntary activities with which they were involved. This was most evident among the very interested group, but was also reported by young people in the two other groups. Unlike the uninterested groups, these young people are more open to receiving information about politics. Indeed, the selectively and very interested groups are often proactive in their acquisition of political information.

In contrast, the generically interested young people tend to be passive recipients of information about politics. Their views and beliefs about politics are still at an impressionable stage, so they are likely to be influenced by those around them. Their views and conceptions of politics therefore have the potential to fluctuate, depending on the nature and consistency of the influences they encounter.

Among those with an interest in politics, the news, particularly television coverage but also press reports, was often identified as a source of information about politics. In addition to this, other political coverage on the television or radio was also sometimes mentioned. For example, young people with a selective interest in politics additionally took an interest in programmes which specifically focused on their issue of concern. Owing to their intrinsic interest in politics, young people in the very interested group, reported listening and following a range of political/current affairs programmes, like 'Newsnight' and 'Question Time', as well as following coverage of political events in the newspaper.

Interest in politics for the selectively interested has been initiated by concern for a particular issue, and they are likely to be open to receiving information and be more knowledgeable within these areas. Apart from

this, however, they are likely to behave in a similar manner to the uninterested groups and may 'switch off' when politics is mentioned. As a consequence of this, they often share similarly negative perceptions of politics and, more particularly, politicians. This, in turn, has reinforced their conception that, apart from the issues that are of concern to them, politics lacks any relevance in their lives. It is therefore possible that if they perceive that their issues of concern are failing to be addressed, their interest might wane in the future.

Interest in politics for the generically interested group has often been activated by changing life circumstances. These have exposed a young person to a range of new influences, including friendships or partnerships, through work or education, but also provoked a reason to take an interest in politics, such as having tax deducted from a first wage packet or when required to fund their courses in higher education. Underpinning their reason for taking an interest was often a range of new roles and responsibilities, arising from familial and economic independence. Interest had also been kindled as a result of a young person having the opportunity to vote. Otherwise, it was said, they had taken interest when a news story had attracted their attention, as in times of international unrest, for example, during the Kosovo crisis.

As previously noted, the very interested group have a more sophisticated and developed understanding of politics, which has been shaped and informed by a range of different sources. In general they are likely to have engaged in some political discussion at home, with one or both parents. In addition, they are likely to have received some kind of political education, either at GCSE or Standard Grade level, or in further or higher education. They may also choose to read books related to the subject, sometimes associated with a course they are studying, for others through general interest.

Alongside this they may also have been engaging in discussions with friends or other people in school or college. The combination of these different sources seems to foster a conception that politics is certainly of relevance and of interest to them. It also ensures they are open to receiving or seeking information about politics. However, because this group have a more sophisticated understanding of politics, they are also likely to be more discerning about the nature of the information received.

The stimulant for their interest in politics varied. In some cases it had been a politically active parent, sibling or other family member who had activated their interest. For others it was their formal political education and a teacher at school, or a particular course, which had inspired their interest. Others said their interest had been kindled following a specific political event, such as the war in Bosnia, or through the influence of a significant other person.

As has been seen, the process in which young people develop and form an interest in politics is fluid and cyclical. It is, therefore, possible that, depending on age and life circumstances, an individual may move between groups as their awareness and interest in politics evolves and develops. For example, it is possible that members of both the politically uninterested groups, but particularly the first group, will acquire and develop an interest in politics. Equally, failure to respond to the concerns of the selectively interested may diminish their levels of interest in politics. Because the generically interested are still at an impressionable stage they have the potential to move in either direction, depending on the circumstances and influences around them. Of all the groups the final group, with their keen interest and awareness of politics, are likely to remain the most static.

4 Images of politics, Parliament and politicians

This chapter examines young people's images of politics, Parliament and politicians. It provides an insight into how young people conceive of politics and political institutions, questions that have received relatively little attention in earlier research. Although existing research shows that young people find politics irrelevant and boring – and hold politicians in low esteem – there is less understanding about why such negative views are held, or the contexts in which they are framed.

Conceptions of politics

Coverage of politics

There were broadly three types of responses to the term 'politics'. The first was a rather vague blankness, evident among those with a low interest in politics, particularly the youngest participants. It was claimed that the word 'politics' brought nothing to mind, and, in some instances, that they had never heard the word before. Even among older participants with little interest in politics there was generally a very limited understanding of what it involved – beyond a broad notion that politics was to do with the Government or the running of the country.

> I don't know what politics is. It's just one of those words, it just sounds [like] it's to do with the Government.
> (Female, 15 years, Indifferent)

A second, and much more common response, was to associate politics with traditional party politics in Britain and the Prime Minister, Parliament, government, politicians and political parties were mentioned. Politics was framed in these terms by young people of different ages, almost irrespective of their level of interest in politics. This would suggest that Bhavnani's (1991) finding that people equate politics with British party politics applies to a wider population than just the young working class.

The third type of response contained broader ideas of what politics attempted to achieve and the issues it addressed. These wider conceptions of politics were found among those with higher levels of interest in politics, but were also evident throughout other groups. Older participants within the indifferent group, for example, associated politics with taxes and the budget, particularly the price of drinks, cigarettes and petrol. In some instances they also related politics to issues such as health, employment and education. Similarly, some in the cynically uninterested and selectively interested groups thought politics involved discussions about 'our lives', taxes, international relations, laws, government allocation of resources and the country's welfare. These participants viewed politics as being connected to money, power and control.

Amongst the interested groups, some felt it covered all areas of life and, as one person said, 'takes you from the cradle to the grave'. Others said politics 'covered everything', all issues and people, and gave specific examples of how it does this.

> Politics affects every section of our lives. It's easy just to see it as employment or tax ... But even [on] the really small-scale, politics in every way

can affect us. (Female, 20 years, Generically interested)

Amongst those with a broader conceptualisation of politics, some viewed politics positively, as a means of representing views and realising hopes. Others had more negative associations, related particularly to short-term planning, control and corruption. Indeed, some people suggested that politicians were responsible for controlling people's lives, although not necessarily in their best interests. There was also some cynicism that politics was mainly about political parties trying to win power, rather than any concerns about societal issues.

It rules our life, society; everyday life is dominated by politics ... Well, theoretically they're [politicians] supposed to represent the people of their constituency in Parliament. But they don't ... They represent their own views, very rarely a local issue gets taken to Parliament and if it does, it's so poor a turnout, you know, it becomes irrelevant. I think most of all they – well, it's a party thing, it's not the individual MP, they're there to build up the party numbers, seats in Parliament. (Male, 21 years, Very interested)

Image of politics

With the exception of those with higher levels of interest in politics, there was an overarching representation of politics as boring and dull. In some cases young people were unable to expand on this view, largely due to a lack of awareness and knowledge. Indeed, the mere mention of the word was enough to make them 'switch off' or make their 'mind go blank'. Others, however, justified their perception, explaining that politics was of relevance only to

certain locations, such as London or England, or to particular groups, such as older people or businessmen. There was also a view that politics entailed cycles of repetitive arguments, with little resulting change.

I think of it as mainly pretty boring. I don't really care about it all that much ... You're always getting different people saying they're going to do this and that whatever, and nothing happens, nothing really changes. (Male, 16 years, Cynically uninterested)

For selectively interested people, the drab image of politics stemmed more from seeing it as inapplicable or irrelevant to their lives or being 'out of touch' with the younger generation. It was even described as a 'headache' because there was too much of it on TV and everything was made into an issue in politics.

Among the generically interested, only the youngest members viewed politics as boring. This was related to a lack of knowledge about politics and a notion, mainly picked up from the television, that politics entailed endless arguing. The older participants, over 18 years, shared this image and sometimes felt that politics did not actually make much difference, although they did not describe politics as boring.

Inevitably, the very interested young people regarded politics as exciting because it provided an opportunity for change. Others, however, were less enthusiastic because they were cynical about whether it would result in change.

Margaret Thatcher and privatisation changed basically the whole structure of profit sector and Tony Blair now is re-structuring, like devolution and reforms like what he's done with the Lords

... For me, it's like big things like unemployment ... and then you go through your recession and you then have a boom and stuff like that ... For me politics is enjoyment (Female, 20 years, Very interested)

Conceptions of Parliament

Physical environment

In general, impressions of Parliament were generated through television broadcasts. Young people consistently described Parliament as a large room with wooden furniture and green leather seats. In addition, some alluded to it being 'big' and 'old', with 'long corridors', 'large halls' and 'meeting rooms'. While the tradition and grandeur of the building was admired sometimes, there was also felt to be something strange and antiquated about the environment of the Houses of Parliament.

Those who had visited the Houses of Parliament, either with school or on a tour, recalled the large scale of the building, as well as the restricted access to some parts. There was also some discussion of the available facilities, such as bars and restaurants. Some surprise was also expressed at how empty it appeared. Among those who had not been to the Houses of Parliament there was a perception that it was closed to the general public.

Location of Parliament

The physical location of Parliament reinforced a feeling of remoteness for young people outside London, but particularly for Scottish and Welsh participants. Scottish participants reported that the geographical distance of Parliament contributed to their feeling of being marginalised by the Westminster Parliament.

The way in which this restricts the access that young people can have to politicians and Parliament was emphasised. It was also said that this further limits their opportunity to become involved in the political process.

Function of Parliament

To aid discussion young people were shown a postcard of the Houses of Parliament. Not everyone, however, recognised this and some of the younger people thought it might be a court, church or hotel.

I've seen it [Houses of Parliament] *somewhere, like on the news or something, is it? London, is it? ... I've seen the clock on the news. I've seen it before but I don't know what it is ... Is it a hotel? People go on holiday there.* (Male, 15 years, Indifferent)

Virtually all of those who lacked an interest in politics were uncertain about what went on inside Parliament. Those with a more developed interest viewed it as a place for debating, making laws and deciding how to improve the country. Some also thought that further activities would take place, such as administration and research. But there was also a general feeling that there were other more secret activities taking place.

The predominant image of Parliament was of politicians arguing and shouting at each other during parliamentary debates seen on television. They described this in various terms such as politicians 'blabbering on', 'huffing and puffing', 'ripping and digging', 'slagging each other off', 'back biting' and 'bickering'. Some of the participants felt that the general public is only given a limited impression of Parliament, as only one room is ever shown on television, leaving the public with a stereotypical image of the arguing.

When you see it on telly though it just looks like a big joke. I mean like the way they carry on in the House of Commons ... You wouldn't even get kids in a school carrying on like that ... with them screaming, and folks sitting in the benches sleeping. (Female, 23 years, Cynically uninterested)

I think there's a lot of kind of personal attacking and not enough real constructive stuff going on ... It's just one big zoo of animals. (Male, 18 years, Very interested)

There were varied opinions about the content of parliamentary debates. Some thought they were 'grey' and boring, or about 'nothing' and never 'get anywhere' because issues are never resolved. Impressions were sometimes based on politicians themselves looking bored.

On TV you can see all of them sitting there ... half of them's falling asleep. With the way they look you only have to take one look and you think 'turn over'. They're like me they find it boring ... If they're nodding off then it must obviously be boring. (Female, 21 years, Indifferent)

Others found the debates bewildering and daunting, as there seemed to be lots of shouting and noise with little accompanying explanation. Their impression was one of confusion and they found it difficult to understand the proceedings.

Those who enjoyed the debates appreciated the opportunity to hear different viewpoints, or found it entertaining to watch politicians shouting at each other. They found it conveyed a less serious and formal impression of politics, especially when the politicians made jokes about each other.

Sometimes it [Parliament] is quite entertaining to watch ... It's just like the two most important people in the country just arguing and ripping each other to shreds basically ... It gives a kind of unserious edge to politics as a whole, rather than if it was all very formal and serious then you'd probably be given a distinct image of politics as being formal and serious. (Male, 16 years, Cynically uninterested)

References were also made to the traditional and ceremonial aspects of the proceedings in Parliament. For those with the least interest in politics, this reinforced the unfamiliarity and strangeness of parliamentary proceedings; amusement was expressed at seeing a politician 'flinging a mace round his head', and a vision of a woman shouting "Order" and banging a hammer. Those who were more interested also commented on the 'pomp and ceremony' of Parliament, which they found difficult to understand, irrelevant, old fashioned and a waste of money. Only a small minority felt the ceremony and 'fancy dress' gave the proceedings a sense of dignity and tradition.

Image of politicians

In general, young people viewed politicians as white, male and as either old or middle aged. Whatever the stated age – and there was some variation – it was consistently felt that the age of politicians removed them from young people, and this was indicated by such descriptions of politicians as 'old fogies' or 'coffin dodgers'.

Politicians were also perceived as being wealthy and were generally described as 'posh'. Some also thought that politicians came from the upper classes, or 'good backgrounds'. This, it was said, was demonstrated by their expensive cars and 'big houses' in which they live. As a reflection of their perceived wealth, the politicians were almost universally described as having a smart appearance.

In some cases young people thought they would have been educated privately and attended universities such as Oxford and Cambridge. This impression had resulted in some young people believing they were 'snobby', 'stuck up' and 'think they know everything' whilst others viewed them as 'educated' and 'intelligent'. Among the very interested group, education and intelligence were felt to be necessary requirements for being a successful politician.

The image of a 'yar boo' style of politics in London, as described by Scottish young people, was based on a belief that politicians were typically English. As a consequence, politicians were perceived as being less able to relate to Scottish issues and concerns.

Perceptions of politicians' personalities were variously expressed, often using negative language, such as, 'boring' or 'grumpy' or, in rarer instances, words such as 'evil'. The 'Spitting Image' puppets of politicians were recalled by some of the participants and thought to be both accurate and very entertaining. The young people were sometimes also less than complimentary about the appearance of politicians, describing them, for example, as fat or wimpy, bald or with badly curled hair and big noses. Some held images of politicians eating lots of food and drinking alcohol.

I think it [a politician] *would be a person, probably a man, sitting on a chair with his feet up on a table, smoking a cigar … and having a cocktail.*
(Female, 16 years, Indifferent)

It was also generally believed that politicians behaved in a 'childish' manner in Parliament; not appearing to listen to one another and attempting to 'score points' off each other. This behaviour was viewed by some as counter productive to obtaining a balanced and reasoned opinion.

Those with the least interest in politics were unsure what politicians did, as they never watched or listened to media reports. Others were able to offer suggestions about the role of politicians, and consistently negative functions were described. Despite these perceptions, some individuals, particularly those with greater interest in politics, offered more positive views of politicians. In exceptional cases, young people qualified their statements expressing their difficulty judging politicians because the public only see 'one side' of them, or only have opportunity to see them in certain settings.

Four main areas of criticism are discussed below, together with some of the young people's suggestions for what would make a good politician and their rare positive viewpoints.

Untrustworthy

There was a strong belief that politicians cannot be trusted. It was stated recurrently that they lied and failed to keep their promises. In television interviews, it was claimed, they avoided answering questions and never gave straight answers. In some cases it was thought that they used the media to manipulate their public image, by presenting a selective image. They were, therefore, likened to actors.

… Whenever they do an interview they always seem kind of like … they're just doing it to try and

win some publicity and then they'll go back to their nice little house on the hill afterwards ... (Male, 16 years, Cynically uninterested)

In addition, media reporting of scandals left the impression that politicians were sometimes hypocritical, in advocating good behaviour for others and yet not living up to these standards themselves. They consistently referred to the sleaze and scandals that were reported about politicians in the media as evidence of their bad characters.

Some young people, however, felt there were politicians with integrity and who keep their promises. It was also said that inevitably politicians need to become 'good talkers' and possibly even slightly corrupt in order to achieve anything in politics. Individuals also suggested that the media were largely responsible for the images people held of politicians, in particular through the stories presented in newspapers. It was said that the media obsessively focused on the private affairs of politicians.

When asked what makes a good politician, young people generally thought that honesty was an essential quality. They expressed the belief that good politicians would 'be themselves', keep promises and avoid what were termed 'shady deals'. Good politicians would also give straightforward answers to questions and be publicly accountable for their activities.

Self interested

Another general conception was that politicians do not care about the country or its people, but are merely concerned with being elected.

Most of them don't even care about what happens in Britain; most of them just want to get

in there and try and do what they want ... It's not for the benefit of the country. (Male, 15 years, Indifferent)

It was said with some frequency that politicians do not take their positions seriously and are only in politics to benefit from the system by, for example, changing laws to suit themselves, or to secure public money. It was also said that they only helped members of the public in order to further their own recognition and appeal. There was a general feeling that politicians were overpaid and in addition received too many perks, such as holidays abroad, sometimes at the expense of the tax payer.

Less typically some young people believed politicians were conscientious and have some underlying belief or passion about their work. These people argued that politicians are concerned to represent the public and to improve conditions within society. The hard work required to get into politics was acknowledged, as was the difficult nature of the work, which sometimes requires them to make personal sacrifices. It was also suggested that the high salaries were to compensate them for being in the media 'spotlight'. Others thought that politicians do care initially, but once they have to toe the party line they are 'moulded' into a different way of thinking, and initial ideals and convictions are sometimes forgotten.

It was felt that a good politician would be someone who wanted to improve conditions in society and raise standards of living.

Ineffective

There was a general view that politicians did not achieve sufficient outcomes which benefit the population. This impression was based on the lack of visible changes and the amount of money spent on unnecessary projects, such as the Millennium Dome. There were two main reasons why politicians were thought to be ineffective. First, they do nothing but 'sit on their backsides'; and, second, they talk 'rubbish', 'waffle' and argue 'round in circles' over pointless matters. The lack of unity between politicians, and the level of argument, was also considered to be counter productive to achievements in politics.

Well they [politicians] *just can't make a decision basically ... they just pass the buck all the time ... they're* [always] *arguing ... even in the same groups they never stick together. There's always someone else saying look I don't wanna do it like that. You know they're supposed to be one party so they're supposed to agree on everything ... but it seems like they can never agree.* (Male, 21 years, Indifferent)

However, there were those who felt that politicians were engaged in important work, making decisions for the country and changing things for the better. For example, it was claimed this was evident in the operation of the police force and health service, for example. It was also said that the nature of their work made it impossible to please everyone with their actions. In addition, it was recognised that politicians sometimes do good work that may not be visible to the public. Argument was also sometimes seen to be an inevitable part of the political process. Indeed, there was a view that an ability to debate, stand up for ideals and defend opinions was essential to be a good politician.

Remote and unrepresentative

The perceived age gap and different social background led young people to regard politicians as remote and inaccessible.

It was also consistently claimed that politicians were hard to understand because of the remoteness of the topics they discussed, but also because they confused young people with their jargon, big words, facts and figures.

Politicians were believed to have no understanding of the needs and concerns of the young. They were also felt to be out of touch with 'ordinary' people from different backgrounds and, as a result, were not aware of 'real world' problems and circumstances. Figure 3 (overleaf), drawn by one young person, clearly illustrates the perceived relationship between politicians and young people.

I think politicians are completely separate from society. I don't think they have any connection at all, because I don't feel I've got a connection towards them. They are in grey suits ... and they use big words, long structures and are very long winded. (Male, 20 years, Selectively interested)

The politically uninterested groups were particularly critical of the way politicians ignore the views and concerns of young people. Where politicians did consult them, it was felt that they might only pretend to listen, or only listen to views they want to hear.

The remoteness of politicians was particularly emphasised by young Scottish people. They discussed the way in which the Westminster Parliament is dominated by English MPs and, as a consequence, unfairly advantages English and Welsh interests over Scottish interests. It was said, for example, that specific policies, such as care for the elderly and local recreational facilities for young people, were directed more favourably towards the English and Welsh. While the lack of Scottish representatives was raised in relation to all Scottish people, it was mentioned with specific regard to young people.

Nevertheless, there were some who felt that existing politicians are concerned to address important issues and do try to represent the voice of people by fighting for their rights. There was also a view that it is not important for politicians to be interesting as long as they are making important decisions.

Universally, the young people felt that a good politician would be approachable, easy to relate to and would take account of the public's views. In particular, it was believed that a good politician would represent the views of the young, as well as those of older people. In addition, it was felt that a good politician would be someone more 'like themselves'; a younger person or someone who had grown up in similar circumstances to them. Such politicians, it was thought, would be better able to understand and represent their views.

Views of individual politicians

Previous studies (e.g. *State of the Nation Report*, 1998) have documented low levels of knowledge about individual politicians.

Figure 3 An image of a politician drawn by a respondent during one of the focus groups

Note: Respondents were invited to draw a politician in focus groups or paired interviews where young people were having difficulty discussing their images of politicians. This picture was drawn by a young man, aged 18 years.

Although there was no attempt in this study to test levels of knowledge about politics or politicians, it is possible to identify varying levels of awareness. Those who lacked interest in politics mainly expressed views about the current and former prime ministers, Tony Blair, John Major and Margaret Thatcher or party leaders, such as William Hague, Paddy Ashdown and Neil Kinnock. Not surprisingly, those with higher levels of interest referred to a wider range of politicians, including politicians such as Mo Mowlam, Bernie Grant, or Jeffrey Archer. Generally, there was little awareness of politicians representing their local constituency, except for those belonging to the highly interested group. There also appeared to be greater awareness amongst participants living in Scotland and Wales than amongst those in England.

Across the sample, there were contradictory views about the Prime Minister, Tony Blair. Some thought that he was more in touch with young people, as he is younger than other politicians and has children of his own. This was also felt to be reflected in his more realistic lifestyle and apparent sense of humour.

> *I think Tony Blair … is still in touch, he still knows what it is like to live in a normal house and have a family and like having to earn money.*
> (Female, 17 years, Selectively interested)

However, others were cynical about his attempts to appeal to Britain's youth by, for example, inviting celebrities to Downing Street. They also questioned his commitment to young people, citing the introduction of college fees as evidence of this. Television was the main source of their views about Tony Blair but there was also some reference to comments made by family or friends.

Images of the politically interested

In general, young people held the view that politics is of interest to older, rather than younger people. However, what was defined as 'older' varied and shared only the common feature that it meant they were older than participants' current ages. Parents and grandparents were believed to be more interested in politics than their children or grandchildren, because they have 'settled down' and are, therefore, concerned about issues that could affect their families.

There was also a view that people who shared a similar background to politicians were more likely to take an interest in politics, but not people who were 'poor' or 'working class'. It was thought that 'upper class' people would be able to understand politics as it is orientated around things they are concerned about such as finances and fox hunting. The concerns of 'working class' people were felt to be less well addressed by politicians.

People who do well at school or go to university, 'swots' or 'nerds' as they were sometimes called, were considered more likely to be interested in, or to participate in, politics as they would be more capable of understanding and engaging with that world. It was also felt that such people are more likely to be encouraged to take an interest and to participate in politics at school and at home. They were also considered to have less of a social life and therefore have more time to gain information about politics from watching the news and reading the papers.

People who work in politics were inevitably considered to take an interest in politics. Generally, people in good jobs or those paying taxes were thought to also have a vested interest in politics. Businessmen, in particular, were considered to be most interested as they are likely to be affected by politics, in terms of finance and employment issues. In addition, politics was considered to be relevant to teachers or health care professionals, as they would be affected by levels of state funding.

There was also a view that people who were concerned about changing things would be interested and active in politics. Generally, it was felt that these people could be from any social background. There were differing views, however, about such politically active people, with some describing them as 'busy-bodies' and others considering them to be kind and concerned people.

Views about the Scottish Parliament

In general, young Scottish people were either in favour of Scottish devolution or appeared to be indifferent to the prospect of constitutional change. In some cases, indifference resulted from uncertainty, or from lack of knowledge about politics but for others, the reasons were less clear. Only a few people seemed to be directly opposed to the idea of devolution for Scotland and, among those who were eligible, a few had voted against it in the referendum.

Positive views about devolution

A number of arguments were made in favour of devolution. Essentially, these were concerned with two issues. First, there was optimism that this would free Scotland from domination by England and ensure Scottish interests are represented and addressed. Second, it was thought that having an individual identity would give Scotland greater prestige and status as a nation. While these points were raised in relation to all Scottish people, they seemed to have greater poignancy with regard to young people.

> *I like the idea of the Scottish Parliament, because instead of being ruled from London – that wee country up north ... there will actually be Scottish people, in Scotland, doing what is best for Scottish people. (Male, 19 years, Selectively interested)*

There were three ways in which it was felt that their increased representation would be achieved. First, national and local needs would be more responsively addressed and delivered. Second, there would be greater control for Scotland, for example, in terms of management of the economy and the authority to set tax levels and decide on the allocation of resources. It was argued that this increased control was a logical progression since Scotland already has its own education, legal system and currency. Third, it was said that, because politics will become more relevant to Scottish people, they will be encouraged to be more interested and engaged in politics. It was also noted that the Scottish Parliament will provide the opportunity for younger more representative politicians to enter Parliament.

Among these positive views there was some scepticism about whether the Scottish Parliament would be given sufficient powers to be independent from Westminster. In particular, concerns were expressed about the degree to which Scotland will be given the power to raise taxes and to legislate independently of Westminster. There was also some uncertainty about whether Scotland would be able to survive financially without English revenue, particularly as it was acknowledged that North Sea oil will not continue forever.

I think it'll be good for Scotland … but I sort of don't know how much difference they're going to be able to … make. Because they've still got to interact with them down in London. There's just going to be so many limitations on them, they may not be as effective as they'd want to be. I think that would be frustrating for the government and for the country in general (Female, 20 years, Generically Interested)

It's going to be like school prefects … watching you all the time, or Big Brother is watching you. Making sure you are not stepping out of line … I think they might hold us back, make sure we don't get too Scottish. (Male, 18 years, Generically interested)

Caution was also expressed about the time it would take to evolve. There was also a fear that Scottish people are sometimes overly 'romantic' and perhaps even a little unrealistic in their hopes for the Scottish Parliament.

Negative views about devolution

Opposition to Scottish devolution was primarily focused on whether Scotland will be able to survive as an independent country. This point was raised in two ways. First, that Scotland will not be able to sustain independence on a financial level. Second, that Scotland may not be strong enough to defend itself in times of war. Underpinning these views, however, was a desire for Scotland to be a part of the UK.

5 Political engagement

Discussion about the opportunities for political engagement reveal that young people felt powerless and excluded from the political process. When this is considered in the context of their lack of political interest and understanding, it is not surprising that concerns are voiced about the future health of British democracy. However, as will be seen, levels of interest in politics did not always indicate a willingness to engage politically.

Indeed, there is evidence to suggest young people are engaging in a wide range of political activities – irrespective of levels of political interest. It would seem that because of their rather narrow conception of politics, however, they are sometimes unlikely to perceive their action as a political activity. It would also appear that their lack of participation is as much to do with their perceptions about being excluded from politics as it is to do with their lack of interest and understanding of it.

What constitutes a political activity?

Discussion about the ways in which young people can express their views sometimes proved difficult to stimulate, as participants did not necessarily have well-formed views on what constitutes a political activity. In some cases, voting was seen as the only legitimate way in which young people could express their views and take part in politics. Others, however, based their judgement on whether the government would be directly involved in some way. For these people, a political action might involve a range of different methods which included signing petitions, taking part in demonstrations protesting about government policy, joining a political party and lobbying MPs through their surgery or through written correspondence. Whereas others interpreted the definition of political action even more loosely and included any activity which might directly or indirectly be related to politics. Actions in this latter category included joining a union, or pressure group, writing to the Press, and protesting to the local council. Young people in the politically interested groups perceived a wider range of methods for engagement in politics than those in the uninterested groups.

The efficacy of a particular method was principally assessed according to its potential to persuade the government to listen and respond to the message being delivered. The success with which this could be achieved was felt to depend on the number of people who were willing to support a particular action, and the nature and visibility of the message being conveyed. Underpinning these dimensions were two related factors, the weight of the organisation driving the action and the ability to attract media coverage.

Barriers to participating in politics

A number of barriers were identified as having prevented and even excluded young people from participating in politics. Underpinning these, however, was a degree of apathy about politically engaging.

> *It's really easy to be just really apathetic, be lazy about it … If you want to change something you have to be really active. And unless a way of doing that is presented for you, it's really easy to not bother to do it.* (Female, 20 years)

The following barriers were perceived to exclude young people from politics.

The limited number of opportunities that are available for young people to participate in the political process was consistently noted. In some cases young people could not see any conceivable way for them to take part in politics until they reached electoral eligibility. Their feeling of powerlessness was repeatedly emphasised, as was the frustration of having doors closed to them that were open to those who were older.

> They [politicians] *can more or less do what they want to us because we have no power yet to do anything about it.* (Male, 18 years)

> *Being on your own and under age ... you have no way of doing anything.*
> (Male, 16 years)

Even where young people acknowledged there were opportunities to participate in the political process, either through conventional methods, such as voting or lobbying MPs, or less conventional methods, such as youth forums, they felt they lacked knowledge about the process of engagement. Underpinning this barrier was the perception that politics was a complex and alien subject, which they found hard to grasp and understand.

> *Say I wanted to ... do something, like complain about something, I wouldn't know what to do – I think there's very little education about how the system actually is organised* (Male, 18 years)

> *It's just that young people don't seem to [know], nobody goes up to them and says "Ere you go, politics. If you've got anything you wanna know, go and phone them or go and see them", or whatever. It's like at school, if somebody says. If you've got questions about your career, that's*

> *who you can reach to see about it. And they're given that information but there isn't anybody that does the same for politics so they're not going to know.* (Female, 19 years)

It was also consistently argued that the views of young people remain unheard by politicians. Underpinning this view was a perception that politicians often dismiss the views of young people as childish and unrealistic.

> *Even when you're 18/19 they don't listen to you, 'cos they look at you, and think: 'You're young' ... maybe when you're getting to 25, ... got a job and sort of like stature in society ... they'll listen to you more, if you're like the managing director of a big company ... people know about you and listen to you more.* (Male, 15 years, Indifferent)

> *They seem to be making judgements ... and not actually listening to what we're saying, for instance with the funding for the students, there's been uproar and people protesting but you know nothing, no action's taken.* (Female, 22 years, Cynically uninterested)

Instead, it is argued, politicians listen to the views of those with money and status. Whilst it was acknowledged by a few people that, in certain policy areas, such as New Deal for Young People, voices are being heard, there were clearly others, such as education, where their needs were ignored. Because of this lack of interest in their views, young people felt it would require an enormous effort before they would begin to be heard. There was, therefore, some reluctance about expending their energy in politics if it was likely to have so little impact.

Relating to this last point was a common perception that young people lack representation in Parliament. This had been observed, particularly in relation to age, but also for members of different ethnic minorities and for people living in Scotland and Wales.

How are young people engaging with the political process?

Participation in politics did not seem to relate to levels of political interest. If there were a direct relation between interest and activity, then it would be logical to assume that the politically uninterested groups would refrain from engaging politically. As will be seen, although they are more apathetic than those in the interested groups, they are nevertheless sometimes engaging in political activities.

Young people in the politically uninterested groups seem to engage politically when issues have direct personal relevance to them or to their local community. For example, the protection of leisure facilities, such as a skate park, or football pitch, funding for further and higher education, and preventing the closure of a local hospital or school, had resulted in young people signing petitions or attending demonstrations. In addition, a few people had also signed petitions in support of broader moral concerns, such as animal rights. In terms of their voting behaviour, there is evidence of people voting and not voting in both politically uninterested groups. Where the young people are voting, they are more likely to be voting at general rather than local and European elections.

The politically interested groups characteristically involve themselves in a wider range of political activities, including signing petitions, joining organisations and taking part in activities on behalf of these groups, writing to politicians (often in connection with a school project) and taking part in demonstrations. For example, young people were involved in groups supporting animal welfare, human rights or poverty in developing countries. As with the uninterested groups, there is evidence of some voting and some not voting, although there does appear to be some indication that the most committed and regular voters in all elections are those in the highest political interest group.

Responses to the first voting opportunity

As noted in the introduction, the prospect of voting did not necessarily hinge on levels of interest in politics, nor on reported voting behaviour. Some of the young people emphasised the importance of voting, despite the fact that they had not voted or did not intend to vote in the future. There were a number of ways in which young people responded to the opportunity to vote.

Young people conveyed a sense of importance and sometimes even excitement about finally reaching electoral eligibility. Their positive reactions were fuelled by a desire to express a particular view, which they perceived might have the potential to persuade politicians to be responsive to their needs and might also result in a change of government.

I remember going to vote and it was, 'Wow! I'm old enough to vote!' and I was thinking, 'Yes, this will make a change!' ... Finally got a chance to say something ... to take my view forward by putting a cross in the box, yes. 'You're really going to listen to me now, aren't you?' That's what I thought, I felt like I was doing something constructive, and changing something. I don't know what it was, but it was just like you had the power of the voter, kind of thing. Putting a little cross in the box, that's great. (Male, 20 years)

Young people also talked about their duty and responsibility to engage with the democratic process. Underpinning this view was a belief expressed by some that voting brings with it the right to complain and be critical of current political events. By implication, people who refrain from voting forfeit the right to comment. A few young women also described a duty to vote as a debt to the work of the suffragettes.

Other young people appeared to be indifferent to the prospect of voting. Whilst they acknowledged the importance of voting they equally expressed apathy about voting at present. Underpinning this view was the notion that voting was only important for those who were concerned about politics and equipped with the information to make an informed choice. Their apathy stemmed from a perception that politics does not seem to be affecting them and they have not got the information at their disposal to make an informed choice.

The final group was cynical about the importance of voting. Their cynicism was based on a perception that there is no point exercising their democratic right because the views of young people will be ignored. In addition, a few young people alluded to the electoral system, which meant that in certain circumstances they were wasting their vote. This group did not appear to be looking forward to the prospect of voting and those who had the opportunity were not inclined to vote.

Comparisons were made between voting and other freedoms young people were entitled

to, such as drinking, at the age of 18. There were mixed views about the appropriateness of having the vote at 18. For some, having to wait until they were 18 had compounded their feelings of exclusion from the political process. The point was made that, at 16 young people are old enough to have a child, but too young to vote. However, concern was also raised that people under the age of 18 are too impressionable and immature, and should not be given the opportunity to vote. This issue will be revisited in the final chapter.

Voting behaviour at the 1997 General Election

This next section specifically considers voting behaviour in the 1997 General Election. It was sometimes difficult to explore voting behaviour and motivations for this at the individual level because of the use of focus groups within this study.

The role of family and class in voting decisions

The key role of family and class in first voting decisions has long been recognised and reported (see for example, Butler and Stokes, 1969). Within this study, the parental role model typically seems to be guiding voting decisions when young people lack interest and knowledge about politics and where they are still living within the family home. After this, it continues to be persuasive only where young people maintain their lack of interest and knowledge of politics, and are therefore unlikely to be engaged in other influential processes. In general, the parental and family role model is guiding the choice of vote. However, in some circumstances it is additionally playing a role in driving the decision whether to vote or not. There is evidence that some parental pressure is being exercised in order to persuade and sometimes coerce young people, who had not intended to vote. Among this category of voters, were some of the members of those groups who had no interest in politics.

An independent choice

Not surprisingly, once young people have left the parental home, other influences may assume a greater importance and an independent voting choice can be made. However, independent choices were also made by young people still living at home. This occurred mainly where the young people were not receiving cues or information about politics, where there were differing or conflicting views within one family, or when the young person had an interest in politics and, as a consequence, disagreed with the view expressed at home.

Young people who made an independent choice were driven to vote in a particular way for the following reasons:

- The influence of a peer group which had shaped the nature of the vote cast. Young people had either followed the crowd and copied the voting decisions of others around them or, after discussing a particular policy or party, a collective decision had been arrived at to vote in a particular way.

- Disaffection with the Conservatives and the need for a change of government had driven the voting decisions of a number of young people. Voters in this group varied as to whether they were making a positive vote for the Labour party or simply ensuring the removal of the Conservative party from government. Whilst some of these young voters may have been inclined towards the Labour party, the desire to remove the Conservatives from government was uppermost in their minds.

We were really excited by the whole idea, and because we definitely ... thought that – it was so exciting ... that Labour were going to get into power, and the Tories who'd been in power all our lives were going to be chucked ... and we could feel our first vote was quite an influential one. (Female, 21 years)

A few young people indicated they had opted for a tactical vote rather than support their preferred choice of candidate, whom they felt was unlikely to win the election.

- A personal need had persuaded a few young people to arrive at a particular voting decision. These young people were responding to policies which were of personal relevance for them, such as proposed education reforms, the introduction of the minimum wage, pensions and financial policies, which would benefit a young home owner.

- For some young people the novelty of voting for the first time seemed to have been the reason for voting. It had driven some young people to go to the polling station without any clear idea of who they were voting for. Indeed, it was sometimes attributed to the physical appearance of a particular candidate or a completely random decision.

Because I'd just turned 18 and was allowed to vote and I thought, yes, must go down because all my friends had just turned 18 so we went in just to see what it was like. (Male, 20 years)

Voting deterrents

A number of factors were identified as deterring young people from voting. These can be divided into passive and active deterrents.

Passive deterrents

Politics is not of relevance or interest was a key reason why young people in the uninterested groups had not voted. Their general apathy towards voting was driven by their boredom with it as a subject and a preoccupation with other issues. Indeed, some young people confessed to lacking the desire to take an interest in politics, or notice of when an election was held. Others rationalised their decision with the idea that millions of other people will be voting and so their vote is unlikely to matter.

A related justification for not voting was that they lacked understanding about politics. These young people claimed they were uncertain about who to vote for and did not have enough information at their disposal to make an informed choice. An unwillingness to vote for an unknown candidate was exceptionally underpinned by a concern that their ignorance might result in an unfavourable candidate or party being elected.

Registration issues also resulted in some young people not voting. Some had decided not to register, others had registered but, because of their transient lifestyle, found themselves in the wrong place on polling day. It was also said that there was some reticence about joining the electoral roll because it would result in payment of the council tax. A final way in which registration issues were discussed was in relation to people being barred from voting because they were not British citizens, despite having been brought up in Britain.

Active deterrents

A lack of trust and faith in politicians to tell the truth and keep their promises was reported as being a disincentive to vote.

The idea that young people's views are ignored by politicians had also dissuaded young people from voting. It was said that there was little incentive to vote because politicians fail to take an interest in the views of young people.

The inability to affect the outcome of the election was acknowledged as having put a few people off voting. The belief that a party was unlikely to win in a particular constituency where another party was dominant, had persuaded people to refrain from voting.

Finally, because there appeared to be so many similarities between the Conservative and Labour party, it was also believed that there was no opportunity to bring about change or make a difference to the way the country is governed and, therefore, no point voting.

6 Encouraging political interest

This final chapter draws together some of the key themes raised throughout the report and considers their implications for future action. As a prelude to this, the proposals which young people put forward for engaging greater interest and participation in politics are summarised.

The suggestions young people made for encouraging political interest centred on the factors that were turning them away from politics. They were therefore concerned with three related areas: making politics more interesting and accessible; making politicians more responsive to the needs and concerns of young people; and finding new opportunities and routes for young people to enter the political process.

Among the initiatives recommended some are already in place, although not sufficiently apparent or successfully enticing young people; others are new suggestions, not all of which may be feasible or appropriate. A number clearly accord with plans for citizenship training.

Making politics more interesting and accessible

If young people are to become more interested in politics they need to be persuaded that the subject has greater relevance within their lives. It also needs to be delivered in a more enjoyable and entertaining way than at present.

Politics therefore needs to be framed in terms which resonate with the issues and concerns of young people. Emphasis should therefore be placed on illustrating the different ways in which politics affects the lives of young people and, through this, demonstrating that issues which are of concern to them are being addressed, and responded to, by politicians. It was suggested that finding an alternative label to 'politics', such as 'culture' or 'social issues' might be an initial way to overcome negative and narrow preconceptions about the subject.

Turning to the way in which politics should be delivered, young people implied that a balance needs to be struck between delivering politics in a lively and enticing way without trivialising or withholding important information. Care should also be taken to ensure that information is delivered in a neutral and impartial way. The vocabulary used needs to be easy to understand, using words which are simple and devoid of jargon and technical language, but without patronising.

School and the media were the two key ways discussed for delivering information about politics. It was argued that both these channels would have the potential to contribute to levels of knowledge and understanding. Views about each method varied and there were some who did not believe either would be worth pursuing, because politics was just too 'boring' and 'complex'.

> *It's just ... not an interesting subject, people don't sit with their popcorn and a few cans of beer in front of the telly and watch Question Time very often ... Very few people find it interesting ... It's inherently dull ... I can't see how you could make ... the administration of the Water Board or something ... interesting at all. The relationship of quangos to that policy-making process – you'd much rather be watching football, wouldn't you?*
> (Male, 21 years)

When asked about the aspects of politics that they wanted covered, young people sometimes suggested the very areas they claimed were turning them off politics. Inevitably there were variations in the level and sophistication of the information required. Their suggestions for coverage were of three kinds. First, the need to explain what politics is and to demonstrate how it affects young people using illustrations of relevant political issues. Second, finding a way to equip young people with information about the political process; of particular interest were, the role of individual politicians, party politics and the legislative process. Third, to explain to young people how to vote and, for members in the high interest group, how different voting systems operate.

Teaching politics at school

Discussion about the need for political education was concerned with whether it would improve levels of understanding and interest in the subject. Some young people argued it was being taught with varying effect, but others felt it was far too boring to be taught at school. However, it was acknowledged that even if young people had not appreciated the benefits of being taught courses, such as French, at the time they, nevertheless, found them helpful later. In the same way they reasoned that politics might be of use to them in the future.

Judgements about the appropriate age to introduce political education related to concerns about the difficulties that young people may have in understanding politics. Some argued that politics should be gradually incorporated from primary school onwards, whereas others suggested either just before or after 16 years.

There was also some debate about the merits of making politics a core subject. While some young people were resistant to the idea of politics being a compulsory class, it was equally recognised that few people would opt for it otherwise. As an alternative, it was suggested that politics could be incorporated as part of an existing course, such as history or sociology.

Emphasis was placed on delivering politics in an interesting and entertaining manner by, for example, using visual aids such as pictures and videos. In addition, it was suggested that lessons could be made interactive through the use of discussions, quizzes and inviting guest speakers to give presentations. Extracurricular activities, such as visiting Westminster, were also suggested.

Informing through the media

Discussion about the media was primarily concerned with the use of television as the key medium[1], although young people did talk about channelling information through a range of popular outlets such as teenage magazines, computers and the Internet.

Various suggestions were made about how politics could be delivered on television. Naturally, the key issue for maintaining attention was that it should focus on issues which are relevant to young people. Specific suggestions about the format were concerned with involving young people in the programme, either on location or in the studio, on panels or through interviews. Other ideas involved showing young people how they are affected by a particular issue, such as the NHS. It was also suggested that politics could be incorporated in chat shows and soap operas. Otherwise their suggestions involved using humour, with the aid of comedians, such as Rory Bremner or Freddie Star. Celebrity presenters, such as the band, Oasis, presenters from the 'Big Breakfast', actors, such as from 'Friends' or 'Eastenders', were also commonly suggested as potential role models for young people to learn about politics.

Other ideas were concerned with making political coverage less 'newsy' either by changing the setting or removing the backdrop of Parliament – and not focusing on 'boring' politicians 'droning' on. However, irrespective of the format, it was said that the word 'politics' should be avoided as far as possible. Young people also talked about the need to use simple and plain English, to give a balanced perspective, but without overwhelming audiences with unnecessary detail. Finally, it was said that the style of delivery should not be prescriptive, but should enable young people to arrive at their own views and conclusions.

Changing politicians

The young people wanted politicians to be more responsive to their needs and interests. They were concerned to remove the mystique shrouding politicians, in order to make them seem less stuffy and remote. Discarding the formal 'power suits', abandoning the pomp and ceremony, removing the wigs and gowns, and avoiding the antiquated and formal turn of phrase were some of the ways in which it was suggested that this could be achieved.

> *It puts me off ... that's not a normal person that dresses like that ... that was way back when it first started, I think that should be stopped. I can't see the point of wearing all those wigs and cloaks.* (Female, 16 years)

It was said that if politicians were to command the respect and trust of young people, they needed to be more genuine, honest and committed to keeping their promises. However, there were mixed views about whether politicians should promote a more humorous and friendly persona. There were those who felt that politics is a serious subject and that politicians should act in an appropriately solemn manner. A few even thought they might be suspicious and less trusting of politicians who were overly friendly, humorous and 'trendy'. Others, however, were keen for politicians to inject a bit of humour and lightheartedness into their roles.

It was believed that the interests of young people would be more effectively represented if there were a wider cross-section of politicians, in terms of age, sex, ethnicity and social class. The need for younger politicians, as young as their early 20s, was particularly emphasised, in order to ensure young people were more effectively represented. However, some expressed concern that politicians need to be of a certain age in order to command some level of credibility and to attain wisdom and experience. Young people in Scotland hoped that the Scottish Parliament would provide the opportunity for younger, more representative, Scottish people to become politicians.

It was also felt that politicians in general should make more effort to consult young people and involve them in their policy decisions. Their suggestions focused on ways of ensuring politicians were visibly involved in the local community, for example, by taking part in 'a politics fun day', giving talks in schools, attending local meetings or participating in discussion groups similar to the ones young people had participated in during this study.

New opportunities for young people to participate in the political process

A number of suggestions were made for engaging young people in the political process. These were concerned with bringing young people in contact with politicians, as reported above, lowering the age of electoral eligibility and empowering young people to make their own decisions and to take responsibility for issues which directly affect them.

Lowering the voting age

Some young people believed the only way to engage them would be to lower the voting age to 16. Views, however, were divided about the merits of such a suggestion and arguments revolved around whether young people are capable of making an informed voting choice at the age of 16. It was reasoned that young people could not be relied upon to act responsibly at this age because they lack political awareness. Others were concerned about young people being too immature and impressionable at this time.

With the exception of a few young people, the main opponents to lowering the voting age were aged 18 years and over. Experience of having arrived at, or passed, the age of electoral eligibility had resulted in a realisation that even 18 may be too young to make an informed decision.

> You're still a child when you're 16, 17. ... They wouldn't know what they want, they really wouldn't understand – well I'm 23 and I don't understand ... I just think 16 is too young.
> (Female, 23 years)

Proponents of lowering the voting age

emphasised that it would empower more young people and provide an incentive to take an interest in politics. It was also said politicians would devote greater time and interest in the concerns of young people, even if it were only to secure their vote. Sometimes young people argued in favour of the idea only with the proviso that there should be compulsory political education prior to having such an opportunity.

Alternative ways of empowering young people

Other suggestions were concerned with giving young people some control over aspects of their lives, so as to learn about civic responsibility and decision making. The experience of sitting on a schools council or youth forum was felt to encourage young people to take responsibility for some of the issues which affect them, even if it did not result in contact with politicians. Concern, however, was registered that these forums have the potential to raise expectations, on the part of young people, which sometimes cannot be met. It was said, for example, that the failure of politicians to respond to recommendations from a youth forum had increased individual cynicism and apathy about politics.

Concluding remarks

In the absence of the necessary evidence, it is not possible to assess whether young people are more disenchanted with politics than their predecessor generations. Nor is it possible to judge the implications that such trends might have on the future health of democratic practice in the UK. Indeed, it could be argued that the

43

concern about the so-called 'democratic deficit' is misplaced. Clearly, the notion that young people acquire an interest in politics with age and life circumstances still has considerable currency. It may be, however, that the age at which this is activated is now delayed, as a result of the changing social and economic environment in which young people now live.

Irrespective of this debate, however, it is evident that young people have depressingly low levels of political interest and knowledge. They also have very poor opinions of politicians and parliamentary behaviour. It is also clear that these findings are not unique to the UK. Rather than complacently waiting to see whether their interest in politics grows with time, further investigation is required about the reasons why this occurs, and whether there is scope for actively engaging their interest from an earlier age.

In this context, this study set out to contribute to understanding of young people's political views and behaviour. In order to achieve this, a cross-section of young people, aged between 14 and 24, purposively selected from a diverse range of backgrounds and circumstances in England, Wales and Scotland, were consulted. They were invited to consider politics in their terms, employing their own reference points, as well as conventional political benchmarks.

The research demonstrates that young people cannot be treated as a uniform group where politics is concerned. Not surprisingly, they vary in their levels of interest in politics and display their interest in a variety of ways. But the evidence provides further understanding of how young people assess their interest in politics. It also shows how the interaction between the personal and financial circumstances of an individual, their beliefs and values, and a range of external factors will determine how a young person conceptualises politics, which in turn influences the level of connection they make with politics.

The findings confirm and contribute to existing evidence about the factors that disengage political interest. First, because young people conceptualise politics in a limited and narrow way they perceive the subject as boring and irrelevant to their lives at present. Indeed, it was often said that young people are preoccupied with other interests and activities that dominate their lives and leave little time to devote to politics. Second, their lack of knowledge and understanding about politics, and the difficulties they perceive in trying to grasp such a 'complex' and 'dull' subject, leave them with insufficient access to political matters. Third, their lack of trust in politicians to tell the truth, to keep their promises and be accountable had also turned young people away from politics. Finally, the lack of opportunities for young people to engage in the political process until the age of 18 and the failure of politicians to be responsive to the needs of young people, had also contributed to low levels of political interest.

Evidence in this report has also shown that the issues that concern young people today are by no means narrowly conceived or unilateral. Indeed, they cover the broad political agenda, even if they are framed and spoken about using different terms.

Furthermore, in spite of apparently low levels of interest in politics, young people across the sample had engaged in a range of different activities which were concerned with politics.

Even members of the low interest groups had sometimes voted or taken part in some other activity, like signing a petition or attending demonstrations. Young people, however, consistently referred to the ways in which they are excluded from politics.

As has been shown, the limited and narrow way in which young people conceptualise politics is a key factor discouraging their interest in politics. Young people, however, are not unique in their tendency to equate politics with party politics. What is perhaps heartening is that the solutions which young people suggest will stimulate their interest aim directly at the heart of the problem. That is, they are concerned with ways to bring more interest, relevance and dynamism into politics; to increase knowledge and understanding; to make politicians more responsive; and to open up opportunities for young people to get involved in civic engagement. It is also encouraging that these initiatives emphasise a desire to be consulted and involved in the political process, and not an exclusion from it.

The challenge to those who are keen to kindle political interest is to ensure that young people are aware of the relevance of politics within their lives. They also need to be made aware that politicians' also share a number of their interests and concerns. However, in order to engage their attention politics needs to be delivered in an accessible and enjoyable way that enables them to set aside their boredom with party political squabbles, and to consider and appreciate the issues being discussed. Paradoxically, political parties will clearly have a role to play in achieving this.

The plans to teach citizenship should be applauded, as formal political education clearly has an important role to play. But it is essential that this will operate and coexist alongside the other ways in which young people can be empowered and informed – for example, at home, with friends, at school or amongst the local community and through the media. In addition, politicians clearly need to give more consideration to the concerns of young people; and forums that facilitate such a dialogue and involve young people in the structures and processes of decision making, are required. A number of initiatives for achieving this, such as youth forums, children and youth parliaments, and youth service activities are currently in place and have successfully involved young people for a brief period of time. The call for a Minister of Youth, however, will more permanently raise the profile of young people within central government.

The impact which these initiatives will have, however, depends upon the degree and manner in which young people believe their interests and needs are being heard and responded to. In order to convince young people that their interests will be effectively represented they will want to see politicians from a wider cross-section of society. They will also want to see evidence that politicians are acting on their behalf. Indeed, if expectations are raised and then unmet, this will only serve to increase youth apathy and cynicism. Young Scottish people, for example, expressed high hopes for their increased representation within the new Parliament. But the enthusiasm of some young people may dissipate once they realise that change will be slow to develop and that the composition and style of politics in Edinburgh may not be so different to Westminster. Inevitably, there may also be nothing that can be done to arouse the interest of some young people and they will remain indifferent or uninterested in politics.

In conclusion, a balance needs to be struck between empowering and engaging young people but without pressurising them to take an interest in politics. Young people seem keen to ensure that there are appropriate mechanisms for their involvement, but they may feel increasingly burdened if there are too many requests for their participation. It should be remembered that the electorate as a whole is increasingly being asked to vote in more elections. In addition to general, local and European elections they are also being invited to vote in referenda, or for newly devolved bodies and assemblies. In participating in these elections they are also required to fathom their way through a range of new and complex proportional representation voting systems. Ironically, these moves towards greater participation may be in danger of resulting in what might be termed democratic and civic overload.

Finally, it should be recognised that young people are currently taking action in a range of political activities, even if they do not see them as political. In addition, while they often do not assess themselves as being interested in politics, they are clearly concerned about issues which are at the core of the government's agenda. It would seem that in the past too much emphasis has focused on the apathy of the young. It is now time to focus attention on the role of politicians, educators and elders in engaging and representing the interests of the young.

Note

1   The focus on television may have been stimulated by a task that young people were asked to carry out.

References

Banks, M.H. and Roker, D. (1994) 'The political socialization of youth: exploring the influence of school experience', *Journal of Adolescence,* Vol. 17, pp. 3–15

Banks, M. and Ullah, P. (1987) 'Political attitudes and voting among unemployed and employed youth', *Journal of Adolescence*, Vol. 10, pp. 201-216

Bentley, T. and Oakley, K. with Gibson, S. and Kilgour, K. (1999)*The Real Deal: What Young People Really Think About Government, Politics and Social Exclusion.* London: Demos

Bhavnani, K. (1991)*Talking Politics: A Psychological Framing For Views From Youth in Britain.* Cambridge: Cambridge University Press

Butler, D. and Stokes, D. (1969) *Political Change in Britain.* London: Macmillan

Crick, B. *et al.* (1998) *Education for Citizenship and the Teaching of Democracy in Schools: Final Report of the Advisory Group on Citizenship.* London: Qualifications and Curriculum Authority

Dawson, R.E., Prewitt, K. and Dawson, K.S. (1977) *Political Socialization*, 2nd ed. USA: Little, Brown and Company

Dubois, M. (1980) 'Working paper II, values and attitudes that foster or hinder participation in work and public life', in *The Access of Youth to Work and Participation in Public Life.* Geneva: United Nations

Furnham, A. and Gunter, B. (1987) 'Young people's political knowledge', *Educational Studies*, Vol. 13, No. 1, pp. 91–104

Himmelweit, H., Humphreys, P., Jaegar, M. and Katz, M. (1981) *How Voters Decide.* London: Academic Press

Inglehart, R. (1990) *Culture Shift in Advanced Industrial Society.* Princeton: Princeton University Press

Jowell, R. and Park, A. (1998) *Young People, Politics and Citizenship: A Disengaged Generation?* London: The Citizenship Foundation

Kimberlee, R. (1998) 'Politically apathetic youth: a new generation?', *Renewal*, Vol. 6, No. 2, pp. 87–90.

Mardle, G. and Taylor, M. (1987), 'Political knowledge and political ignorance: a re-examination', *Political Quarterly*, Vol. 58, pp. 208–216

Marsh, A. (1989) *Political Action in Europe and the USA.* London: Macmillan

Mort, F. (1990) 'The politics of consumption' in S. Hall and M. Jacques (eds) *New Times: The Changing Face of Politics in the 1990s.* London: Lawrence and Wishart

Park, A. (1995), 'Teenagers and their politics', in R. Jowell, J. Curtice, A. Park *et al.* (eds) *British Social Attitudes: 12th Report.* Aldershot: Dartmouth

Park, A. (1999), 'Young people and political apathy' in R. Jowell, J. Curtice, A. Park and K. Thomson (eds) *British Social Attitudes, 16th Report.* Aldershot: Dartmouth

Pirie, M. and Worcester, R.M. (1998) *The Millennial Generation.* London: Adam Smith Institute

Richardson, A. (1990) *Talking About Commitment. The Views of Young People on Citizenship and Volunteering.* London: Social and Community Planning Research

Ritchie, J. and Spencer, L. (1994) 'Qualitative data analysis for applied policy research', in A. Bryman and R.G. Burgess (eds) *Analyzing Qualitative Data*. London: Routledge

Roker, D., Player, K. and Coleman, J. (1997) *Challenging the Image.* Leicester: Youth Work Press

Stradling, R. (1977) *The Political Awareness of School Leavers.* Hansard Society: London

Wilkinson, H. and Mulgan, G. (1995) 'Freedom's children', *Demos Paper No.17*. London: Demos

Appendix 1: Technical appendix

A brief description of the study design and conduct is given in Chapter 1. This appendix provides further details of the research methods used in this study. A copy of the topic guide can be seen in Appendix 2.

Research design

As noted in Chapter 1 the study was designed to be qualitative in form in order to permit full and detailed exploration of young people's perceptions of politics. The aim was to ensure young people considered their views about politics in ways that were meaningful to them; and to facilitate the exploration of underlying factors which influenced their levels of political interest and engagement.

A combination of focus groups, individual and paired interviews were employed. Focus groups were used to explore the range and diversity of views and experiences that young people have about politics and the political process. Exposing young people to perspectives of others, within a group setting, helped to refine views and stimulate discussion about subjects which were not always seen as of immediate interest to young people. It also enabled participants to generate ideas and strategies for engaging young people in politics and the political process.

The opportunity to follow up individual views, experiences and behaviour, however, is limited in a focus group as it inhibits interaction between group members. In-depth interviews were therefore used to explore views and behaviour at the individual level. These allowed for example more detailed examination of young people's motivations for choosing whether to engage with the political process.

Previous work carried out with young people at the National Centre for Social Research has shown that young people seem more at ease when being consulted in paired interviews. In view of this, all interviews with young people under 18 were paired (i.e. they were composed of two friends). A similar approach was also adopted for group discussions with young people under the age of 16. In these circumstances smaller group discussions were held (with six rather than eight participants) and each of these was composed of three 'friendship pairs'.

Groups and interviews were structured across four different age bands covering those aged 14–15, 16–17, 18–20 and 21–24 years, which ensured that participants in each were at relatively similar life stages. In the youngest age group, interviews and groups were conducted with boys and girls separately. A total of 193 young people took part.

Sample design and selection

The study focused on two groups of young people: first-time voters at the 1997 General Election and those who will be the next generation of first time voters. It involved young people living in the UK, aged between 14 and 24 years, covering those who were in education, training, employment, or unemployment. The study included a sufficient sample in Scotland to consider issues surrounding devolution.

As this was a qualitative study, the rationale for sample selection was not to select a statistically representative sample of all young people, but to ensure diversity of coverage across certain key variables.

Eligibility for the study was determined

following a complex household screen which was carried out by members of the National Centre for Social Research's survey interviewing panel. Quotas were set in order to prescribe the distribution of the sample selected. These ensured diverse coverage within the specified variables.

In addition to the variables identified in Chapter 1, screening interviewers were asked, where appropriate, to try to include young people from a range of different schools (covering both the state and private sectors). Although household composition was not monitored, a range of different households were featured within the sample and across the different age groups. They included young people living in the family home, living with other unrelated adults, with partners and those who were living alone.

The sample was selected across ten different locations covering a range of geographical areas, including inner city, urban, and more rural and remote areas. In England, the locations were Nottingham, Durham, Farnborough and London. In Scotland, the locations were Glasgow, Edinburgh and St Andrews. In Wales, the locations were Carmarthen and Swansea.

In order to allow sufficient time to monitor the sample distribution and ensure the inclusion of all the key groups specified in the sample design, the programme of fieldwork was structured into two waves.

Seeking parental consent

In accordance with the guidelines that have been developed at the National Centre for Social Research for research with children and young people, parental consent for participation in the research was collected from all parents or guardians of people under 16. For those aged 16 or over, consent was sought directly from the young person involved.

Conduct of the groups, discussions and depth interviews

All interviews and group discussions were exploratory and interactive so that questioning could be responsive to the experiences and circumstances of the individuals involved. In addition, considerable thought was given to the way in which young people should be consulted. This was to ensure that participants felt relaxed and confident about speaking and, in the case of group discussions and to a lesser extent paired interviews, able to resist compliance with any dominant or normative views of their peers.

The study was introduced to young people in general terms – as being about the issues which are of concern to young people aged between 14 and 24. Care was taken to avoid mentioning the word politics as it was presumed that this might constrain the way in which young people approached the subject in the groups and interviews, or might orientate them to consider only conventional images of politics. It was also felt that this was a necessary precaution if the study was to ensure the inclusion of people who have little or no interest in politics.

Members of the research team carried out both the focus groups and the in-depth interviews. The focus groups were carried out in a neutral setting, such as a community or leisure centre, where it was assumed that young people would be less constrained by the physical environment of, for example a school building.

Most of the depth interviews were conducted in participants' homes. A few, however, were conducted in the focus group venues.

Young people were given a small payment (£10 vouchers, £10 or £15 cash depending on their age) in appreciation of their time and any expenses involved in taking part. The focus groups and depth interviews lasted between one and two hours. They were based on a topic guide (see Appendix 2), which outlined the key areas of coverage, but also allowed the opportunity to explore attitudes and experiences in-depth through detailed follow-up questioning. All the groups and interviews were tape recorded after first securing the young person's agreement.

Prior to any mention of politics, the discussions and interviews started by inviting young people to generate a list of issues which were of concern to them. These were then used at different points throughout the groups and interviews as a basis for comparison. They were used to compare the issues which they thought their parents, or people of their parents' age-group would be concerned with; to compare the range of areas they believed politicians were concerned with; and to generate discussion about the ways in which young people can express their views and try to change things.

Considerable thought was also given to finding alternative ways in which to engage young people about a subject that was frequently perceived as boring, complex and intangible. A range of projective and enabling techniques were incorporated into the interviews and group discussions where appropriate. These involved, for example, asking interviewees and group participants to engage in various activities, such as drawing a politician, completing a thought bubble and commenting on a prepared list of strategies.

Irrespective of these different strategies, the group discussions and, to a lesser extent, interviews varied in the way in which participants engaged with the subject. Groups could be characterised as either being lively and easy to stimulate interest, or difficult to arouse interest and discussion.

Analysis of the data

A full set of verbatim transcriptions was produced from the tape recordings of the interviews and the focus groups. The analysis of the interview and discussion material was undertaken using 'Framework', a qualitative analytic method developed at the National Centre for Social Research's Qualitative Research Unit (Ritchie and Spencer 1994) and used in all the Unit's studies.

This method involves the following stages. First, key topics and issues that have emerged from the data, are identified through familiarisation with tapes and transcripts. A series of thematic charts is then devised, and data from each group and interview is summarised and transposed under each key topic. The context of the information is retained and the page of the transcript from which it comes noted, so that it is possible to return to a transcript to explore a point in more detail, or to extract text for verbatim quotation.

This method of analysis is highly flexible in that headings can be changed or amended as required. It also allows an individual case to be followed through or for comparisons to be made between cases. Interpretative analysis is carried out from the summarised material.

The following charts were devised:

- Chart 1: Central chart mapping socio-demographic characteristics alongside a political interest and behaviour profile

- Chart 2: Issues of concern

- Chart 3: Views about politics and politicians

- Chart 4: Nature of interest in politics

- Chart 5: Nature of political activity (except voting)

- Chart 6: Views about voting and voting behaviour

- Chart 7: Strategies for encouraging political interest

In this way the experiences, views and behaviour of all young people have been explored within a common analytical framework, which is both grounded in, and driven by, their own accounts. It has also been possible to detect patterns or associations which occurred among individuals and groups within the study population – such as between those young people who are and who are not interested in politics. In this study, the method enabled the identification of a typology of levels of political interest.

Table 1 Profile of the sample

	Total sample	England and Wales	Scotland
	193	127	66
Sex			
Male	98	65	33
Female	95	62	33
Age groups			
14 – 15 years	52	32	20
16 – 17/18 years	46	29	17
18 – 20 years	46	28	17
21 – 24 years	49	38	12
Social class: groups: 1 and 2			
I	10	7	3
II	21	12	9
IIIN	19	12	7
IIIM	10	6	4
IV and V	14	7	7
Other	16	12	4
Not collected during first wave of data collection	8	5	3
Present activity			
Full-time education	105	69	36
In employment (FT, PT, SE)	50	32	18
Government programme	11	8	3
Unemployed	19	11	8
Something else	8	7	1
Highest educational attainment			
Groups: 2,3 and 4			
No qualifications	17	12	5
Less than five GCSEs A–C/equivalents[a]	27	17	10
Five or more GCSEs A–C/equivalents[a]	47	34	13
Two or more A levels/GNVQs/equivalents[b]	31	18	13
Higher Education qualifications (including HNDs)	16	13	3
Not recorded	3	1	2
Ethnic group			
Black Caribbean	8	8	0
Black African	3	3	0
Black other	7	7	0
Chinese	1	1	0
Indian	4	3	1
Pakistani	7	2	5
White	161	101	60
Not recorded	2	2	0

[a] Five Scottish Standard grades A–C or vocational equivalents.   [b] Scottish Highers or vocational equivalents.

Appendix 2: Topic guide
P5758 political engagement among 14–24 year olds

Aims

To explore:

- how young people view the world of politics – the issues and institutions
- the nature of their interest in politics; and the reasons for their interest or lack of interest
- the nature and source of their political attitudes and interests
- the factors which influence and motivate their engagement or disengagement with the political process
- what would encourage young people to become more politically interested and active.

1. Introduction

- About the National Centre for Social Research.
- To give young people an opportunity to voice their views about the topics/subjects and issues which are important, or of concern to them.
- Project being carried out with people aged 14–24 in England, Wales and Scotland.
- Study funded by Joseph Rowntree Foundation – it is part of a programme of work which is concerned with the views, attitudes, and behaviour of young people.
- Research will be used by government and organisations with an interest in the views of young people.
- Reassure them about confidentiality.

2. Background

- Age.
- Household composition (and current activity of household members).
- Current activity.
- Spare time activities.

3. Issues concerning young people

The aim of this section is to map the issues which are important to young people and identify whether these are different from the issues that are important to older people (their parents and other adults).

Make a list of the issues which arise out of the following discussion.

- What sorts of topics/issues are important or of concern to people of their age today.

  Probe: way in which issues are of concern and reasons why young people care about these issues.

  Examples to help generate topics (only use if need further clarification):

  - some aspect of their lives or the lives of others
  - something which has happened to them or others
  - something which has happened in their local community, nationally or internationally
  - something they would like to change or improve.

  If respondents are finding it difficult to generate a list of concerns or issues, show them a pre-prepared list that contains the following issues: **education**, **drugs**, **racism** and **vegetarianism**. Use these to stimulate discussion, by asking them whether these are issues that are important to them, in what way they are important and whether there are other issues like these that are of concern to them.

- Which of these issues are personally important to them, reasons why, when did they become interested in them.
- If people of their parents age/older people were making this list how would it compare with theirs; reasons why.

4. Image of politics and politicians

- What comes to mind when they hear the word 'politics', what sorts of subjects/ areas does it cover?

  Probe: thinking beyond Parliament – what comes to mind?

  Try to use probes to move beyond conventional politics and explore the boundaries of politics.

- What do they think goes on inside Parliament; reasons why.

Show postcard of Parliament and ask them to imagine they are inside – what is it like inside?

- What do they think politicians do, views about this; reasons why.
- What image do they have of politicians; reasons why.

   Probe:
   - politicians they like/dislike; reasons why
   - any contact with politicians; views about this
   - what makes a good/bad politician; reasons why
   - what sorts of people become politicians; are they like you.

   Use examples if necessary: Tony Blair, Willliam Hague, John Major, Margaret Thatcher.

   If having difficulty discussing image of politicians – give out a piece of paper and get them to very quickly draw a politician – then use these to explore their views about politicians.

- What do they see as being the topics or issues which politicians are interested in or concerned about.

   Probe: how they compare with the topics which are important to them; reasons why/why not.

   Refer back to the list previously created and identify on the list which are political issues.

5. Political attitudes and interest

- How interested are they in politics; reasons why/ why not.

   Probe:
   - what interests them; how they show their interest
   - how they became interested; what has made them take notice or become interested in politics; reasons why
   - changes in levels of interest; reasons why
   - if disinterested – do they think they will become interested; when.

Refer back to the subjects and issues they have just been discussing.

- Do they feel they know what is going on in politics; how do they find out what is going on in politics; how helpful is this information; has this affected their views about politics.

  Probe:
  - where else they find out about politics
  - whether they talk to other people about politics; who
  - what they talk about (people their own age, parents and other people)
  - whether it was talked about at school (i.e. discussions, school trips to Downing Street, taken a course in politics).

Explore how people know politics is so boring when they don't take any interest in it. Often people do not relate their topics of interest to politics, explore why this is.

- What sorts of people are interested in politics; reasons why they are; are they different from people who are disinterested; in what way.

  Probe: people of their age; reasons why/why not.

Use **bubble drawings** in this section – ask them at an appropriate moment to imagine they are watching television and an announcement is made about a new programme called 'left, right and centre' for 14–24 year olds – how would they react – can they write their thoughts about this in the bubble?

6. Political activity and participation

Refer back to the topics and issues which are important to them – take one of their issues and explore.

- How can people of their age/young people get their views heard; are their views heard.
- How easy is it for people to change things; reasons why.

  Probe:
  - people of their age
  - any groups whom it is harder/easier for (e.g. ethnic minority groups).

- What can people do to try and change things (refer back to list); how effective are these methods.

  Probe: other ways of changing things.

Use **show cards** of ballot paper/postcards, protests and vegetarianism to pass round and stimulate discussion about different methods of political action, their effectiveness and to generate other suggestions.

Explore views about voting separately (see section 7).

Probe: *formal activities*, e.g. voting, joining a political party, campaigning for a political party, writing to an MP.

Probe: *informal activities*, e.g. signing a petition, participating in a demonstration, joining or giving money to a lobby/ interest group, e.g. Amnesty International, Greenpeace, other informal political activities.

- Have they ever done anything to try to change things; how effective was this, e.g. something at school or in connection with a local issue.

  Probe:
  - what have they done; reasons why they did this (may need to bring it to local level or issues at school)
  - how effective was this
  - whether done anything else in past.

- Would anything encourage them to do any of the things they discussed, e.g. join a demonstration, sign a petition etc.; reasons why.

- What sorts of people take part in politics, reasons why, are they different from the people who do not take part in politics, in what way.

  Probe: people of their age; reasons why/why not.

7. Views about voting

- Whether they feel closer to any one of the political parties; which one; what is it they like or support; reasons why.

  Probe:
  - how did their feelings develop
  - views about other parties.

- What does/will having the opportunity to vote mean to them, whether they think it is important to vote; reasons why/ why not.

- How much of an obligation is there to vote; reasons why.

For under 18's

- Are they looking forward to voting; reasons why/why not.

  Probe:
  - when will they become eligible
  - will they vote; what; reasons why
  - do they know what they will have to do when they vote.

- What will encourage them to vote, reasons why.
- If there was an election tomorrow how would they vote; reasons why/why not.
- What difference does it make whether young people vote or not; reasons why.
- Do their parents and other family members tend to vote; when and in what way; have they ever talked to them about voting.
- Voting age moved from 21 to 18 about 30 years ago; views about the reasons for this.

For over 18's

Check whether eligible to vote in last general election.

- Whether they have ever voted and when; in what way; reasons why they voted/ did not vote on each occasion.
  - in the 1997 general election
  - in a local election
  - in a referendum
  - in a European election.

For each election where voted:

- How did they decide who to vote for, reasons why.
  Probe: anyone/anything influenced their vote, who/what was this, how it influenced them; reasons why.

- If there was an election tomorrow how would they vote; reasons why.

- When will they next vote; reasons why/why not.
  Explore elections coming up:
  - for Westminster Parliament ; Scottish Parliament/Welsh Assembly
  - for European Parliament
  - local election.

(continued overleaf)

- If they don't vote – would anything encourage them to vote; reasons why.
- Does it matter whether young people vote or not; reasons why.
- Do their parents and other family members tend to vote, when and in what way, have they ever talked to them about voting.
- Voting age moved from 21 to 18 about 30 years ago; views about the reasons for this.

8. Young people, politics and political apathy

Thinking more generally about people of your age …

Write the following sentence on a flip chart using an adjective that relates to the way they have talked about politics e.g. politics *is boring*

Politics is …   *because …*

- What difference does it make if people of their age/young people are/are not involved with politics: reasons why.

  Probe:
  – does it matter whether they take an interest, reasons why.
  – whether feel excluded from politics, reasons why.

Explore why, on the one hand, young people often say they are not interested in politics yet, on the other hand, they seem to be interested in issues that are to do with politics.

- What would encourage people of their age to take an interest in politics, reasons why they would.

  Probe: access to information about politics; if so how and what being taught politics in school; if so how and what opportunity to voice their issues and concerns etc.

Use **show card** of suggested strategies to explore whether these strategies would encourage them to take an interest/get involved in politics.

If they had a one to one with Tony Blair, what would they say and how would they advise him to encourage young people to get more involved with politics.

- Any other issues they would like to raise in relation to young people and politics.